W9-CIJ-866

Coleridge's Nightmare Poetry

Coleridge's Nightmare Poetry

Paul Magnuson

New York University

University Press of Virginia

Charlottesville

THE UNIVERSITY PRESS OF VIRGINIA

First published 1974

Frontispiece: An engraving after Henry Fuseli's painting *Nightmare*

Library of Congress Cataloging in Publication Data

Magnuson, Paul.
Coleridge's nightmare poetry.

1. Coleridge, Samuel Taylor, 1772–1834—Criticism and interpretation. I. Title.
PR4484.M3 821'.7 74-4422 ISBN 0-8139-0534-6

Printed in the United States of America

Contents

Preface

In "My First Acquaintance with Poets," William Hazlitt recorded his impressions of his first meeting with Coleridge, and those impressions reflect, perhaps, the experience of innumerable readers when confronted with Coleridge's poetry. In January 1798 the young Hazlitt accompanied Coleridge six miles on his way from Wem, where Coleridge had been visiting Hazlitt's father, to Shrewsbury. Hazlitt noticed that while expanding on the sacraments, Hume, Berkeley, Bishop Butler, and Paley, Coleridge "continually crossed me on the way by shifting from one side of the foot-path to the other."[1] If Coleridge would only stand still or keep to a steady course, we could all follow him more closely. But approaching Coleridge is not easy; once he is in view and the path toward him marked, he moves, shifting his position and necessitating our setting a new course. Modern scholarship permits us to survey the whole ground, the beginnings and endings of his literary career; and the paths to understanding are multiplied, each by itself insufficient, yet all adding to a comprehension of the patterns of his life.

Following Coleridge's reading has occupied generations of scholars since Lowes's discoveries of some of the sources of "The Ancient Mariner" and "Kubla Khan." While Lowes was temperamentally unwilling to find symbolic meanings in the poems, later critics have been eager to do so, assuming too often that the poetry can be glossed by unveiling the symbols and myths that constitute the sources. One cannot, however, arrive at a definitive understanding of the poems by following the sinuous path of his reading; to do so is to discover only where Coleridge has been, not where he is. One cannot always assume that the images and symbols in Coleridge's poetry always carry with them the particular significance they possessed in the original. Controversies on the value of Kubla Khan's pleasure dome provide a good example. The dome is either the sensual earthly paradise of an Oriental tyrant or Milton's Eden, depending on whether one prefers Purchas or *Paradise Lost*.[2] Establishing sources

[1] Hazlitt, XVII, 113.

[2] See the different positions in House (pp. 119–20), Geoffrey Yarlott, *Coleridge and the Abyssinian Maid* (London: Methuen, 1967), pp. 130–31, and John Shelton, "The Autograph Manuscript of 'Kubla Khan' and an Interpretation," *REL*, 7 (1966), 36–37.

does not resolve the controversy. The Khan's paradise is the property of Coleridge's vision, and to Coleridge it is delightful. Lowes is not to be brought to the bar for fostering such an approach. He was far too wise to attempt a symbolic reading from a study of sources. He well understood the inherent difficulties, especially in so mercurial a mind as Coleridge's, of moving directly from a source study to a statement of meaning.

Another well-traveled road to Coleridge's poetry is the retrospective one, which begins with his later prose and winds its way back to the poetry. But this path, too, has its problems, not the least of which is its length; almost twenty years separate the publication of the poetry and the later prose that is often used to explicate the poetry. Coleridge's theories of symbolism and imagination and the full philosophical and theological context in which he wished to place poetry had not been formulated when the poetry was written. One may even doubt that the theories ever found their full articulation in Coleridge's prose. However that may be, the poetry was not written to exemplify the later program. In fact, he revised the poetry for *Sibylline Leaves* (1817) so that it would more nearly approximate his later theories: the gloss was added to "The Ancient Mariner," the phrase "one Life" was added to "The Eolian Harp," and the "dead calm" in "Frost at Midnight" became the "deep calm."

A third common approach maps the ground immediately surrounding the poem itself, explaining the significance of one image, or set of images, by referring to the particular use of that image, or set, in other poems. Yet to explain one poem by another is to make assumptions about the consistency of symbolism that the poetry will not support. The disputes over Robert Penn Warren's reading of the sun and moon symbolism in "The Ancient Mariner" cannot be settled by arguing that Coleridge consistently used those images elsewhere to represent the understanding and the imagination. Using the same methods, J. B. Beer argues that the sun often symbolizes visionary reason and imaginative insight, not the light of common understanding.[3]

While I have occasionally used each of these approaches, I have tried to subordinate them to one that employs Coleridge's own comments on the poems and concentrates closely on the first versions and the revisions. When the differing texts and Coleridge's explanations

[3]For the highlights of the controversy, see Warren, House (pp. 105–13), Schneider (pp. 252–62), Beer (p. 168), E. E. Stoll, "Symbolism in Coleridge," *PMLA*, 63 (1948), 214–33, and Elliot B. Gose, "Coleridge and the Luminous Gloom: An Analysis of the 'Symbolic Language' in 'The Rime of the Ancient Mariner,'" *PMLA*, 75 (1960), 238–44.

of the poems are studied, his concerns with the problems of the self become clearer. Poetry was for him a process of bringing the "whole soul of man into activity," as he expressed it in Chapter XIV of *Biographia Literaria*. Poetry was the process of creating, and hence knowing, an ideal unified self. The ideal self was, first, to be grounded in an ultimate reality outside the self and, second, to be created by an active mind that brings all of the faculties into play and defines an individuality within the ultimate reality. For the ideal established by this knowledge and creation, I have followed Coleridge's usage and employed the terms *self* and *self-consciousness* interchangeably. His quest for the ideal self finally failed. Coleridge the critic and theologian learned the consequences of failure from Coleridge the man and poet: a mind incapable of seeing itself as anything but an insubstantial shadow. When I have used the terms *self* and *self-consciousness* to refer to the results of his inability to achieve the essential wholeness, the meaning of the terms is clear in the context.

Coleridge's difficulty in realizing the ideal self is first fully evident in his ambivalent attitude toward the "intellectual Breeze" in "The Eolian Harp."[4] In the image of the breeze, there is a conflict between the two aspects of his ideal self. While the breeze provides the ground for his being and an animating energy for the universe, it plays on a poet who is passive. The breeze prevents the poet from being active, the second requirement Coleridge knew was essential for the creation of the ideal self. His major poetry reflects this same ambivalence toward powerful forces, which are frequently regarded as objects of fear because they threaten to overwhelm him. Since Coleridge rejects the image of the harp and the breeze with good reason, I have not attempted a symbolic or sacramentalist reading such as Warren's, which equates Coleridge's symbols with the "intellectual Breeze" or the One Life. External objects that Coleridge at first perceives clearly often become part of a phantasmagoria that reveals, not an independent cosmic order, but the state of his mind. The albatross is at first what the mariners make of it, the one vivid, recognizable object that is familiar to the crew in an increasingly unfamiliar seascape. Furthermore, it is the last familiar object the mariner sees as his mind withdraws in fear into the nightmare. Similarly, the pleasure dome in "Kubla Khan" is primarily a vivid and solid "thing," to use Coleridge's own word for it, which becomes ever more insubstantial and finally vanishes.

Humphry House has wisely observed that if, as Lowes said,

[4] The ambivalence remains throughout Coleridge's later writings. For a discussion of the philosophical issues involved, see McFarland.

"Kubla Khan" and "The Ancient Mariner" are the result of an extraordinarily fertile process of association, Coleridge's "greatest strength and part of his greatest weakness derived from the same mental source. . . . But even apart from those two poems, there can be no question that it was by this swift and facile combination of diverse material from his observation and enormous reading that Coleridge achieved his quite exceptional brilliance as an extempore talker and his fertility of image and illustration." What Lowes saw as the capacity to combine widely different images House saw as destructive: "this very fertility could be suicidal."[5] The phantasmagoria is created through association over which Coleridge has no control. Upon numerous occasions Coleridge's assertions of the power of imagination to create a substantial self are accompanied by an admission that he could not realize that ideal self because of his lack of control of the phantasmagoria. In the course of my argument I will offer readings of those of his major poems that reveal an increasing awareness of his failure to create the self, the resulting fear that gripped him, and the expression of that fear and guilt in dreams. The experiences that Edward Bostetter called the mariner's "nightmare world" were Coleridge's as well.[6]

Anyone writing on Coleridge today owes more debts than he can possibly repay. Professor Kathleen Coburn's magnificent edition of the *Notebooks* and Professor E. L. Griggs's of the *Letters* have been indispensable. The generations of Coleridge's interpreters who provide the contexts of the dialogue in which I participate have been enormously helpful, even though I have not always noted their part in the dialogue. To Professor James Scoggins, who first read the manuscript and always posed challenging questions, I owe particular thanks. For reading portions of the manuscript and for permission to reprint sections from my article "The Dead Calm in the Conversation Poems" in the spring 1972 number of *The Wordsworth Circle* I would like to express my gratitude to Professor Marilyn Gaull.

I am grateful for permission to quote from the following sources: Coleridge's *Biographia Literaria, Collected Letters,* and *Complete Poetical Works* and Wordsworth's *Poetical Works,* by permission of The Clarendon Press, Oxford; *The Notebooks of Samuel Taylor Coleridge,* edited by Kathleen Coburn, Bollingen Series L, vol. 1: Text and Notes, 1794–1804 (copyright ©1957 by Bollingen Foundation); vol. 2: Text and Notes, 1804–1808 (copyright ©1961 by Bollingen Foundation), re-

[5] House, p. 46.

[6] "The Nightmare World of *The Ancient Mariner,*" *SIR,* 1 (1962), 241–54.

printed by permission of Princeton University Press and Routledge and Kegan Paul, Ltd.; *The Collected Works of Samuel Taylor Coleridge,* edited by Kathleen Coburn, Bollingen Series LXXV, vol. 4, *The Friend,* edited by Barbara E. Rooke (copyright ©1969 by Routledge and Kegan Paul, Ltd.), reprinted by permission of Princeton University Press and Routledge and Kegan Paul, Ltd.; *Inquiring Spirit,* edited by Kathleen Coburn (copyright 1951 by Routledge and Kegan Paul, Ltd.); Humphry House's *Coleridge: The Clark Lectures 1951–52* (©1962 Humphry House estate), by permission of Mrs. Madeline House; J. L. Lowes's *The Road to Xanadu* (copyright 1927 by Houghton Mifflin Co. and Constable and Co.); *S. T. Coleridge,* edited by R. L. Brett (©1971 by G. Bell and Sons); *The Works of George Berkeley, Bishop of Cloyne,* edited by A. A. Luce and T. E. Jessop (copyright 1948–57 by Thomas Nelson, Ltd.); *The Philosophical Lectures of Samuel Taylor Coleridge,* edited by Kathleen Coburn (copyright 1949 by Philosophical Library).

The University of Pennsylvania generously granted me summer fellowships for 1970 and 1972 to free me from other duties. I have benefited from conversations with Professor Daniel Harris and Professor Robert Ross and have been saved from many embarrassments by Martha Ledger, who assisted in preparing the manuscript. Finally, my greatest debt is owed to my wife, Bonnie, who suffered my silence and preoccupation, and to my daughter, Elise, whose exuberance often provoked her father's impatience.

Abbreviations

Books

Allsop	[Allsop, Thomas]. *Letters, Conversations, and Recollections of S. T. Coleridge*. New York: Harper, 1836.
Asra Poems	Whalley, George. *Coleridge and Sara Hutchinson and the Asra Poems*. London: Routledge, 1955.
Beer	Beer, John B. *Coleridge the Visionary*. London: Chatto and Windus, 1959.
Berkeley	*The Works of George Berkeley, Bishop of Cloyne*. Ed. A[rthur] A[ston] Luce and T[homas] E[dmund] Jessop. 9 vols. London: Nelson, 1948–57.
BL	*Biographia Literaria*. Ed. John Shawcross. 2 vols. Oxford: Oxford Univ. Press, 1907.
*CL**	*Collected Letters of Samuel Taylor Coleridge*. Ed. Earl Leslie Griggs. 6 vols. Oxford: Clarendon Press, 1956–71.
Friend	*The Friend*. Ed. Barbara E. Rooke. 2 vols. *The Collected Works of Samuel Taylor Coleridge*. Vol. 4. Princeton: Princeton Univ. Press, 1969.
Gillman	Gillman, James. *The Life of Samuel Taylor Coleridge*. London: Pickering, 1838.
Grosart	*The Prose Works of William Wordsworth*. Ed. Alexander B. Grosart. 3 vols. London: Moxon, 1876.
Hazlitt	*The Complete Works of William Hazlitt*. Ed. P[ercival] P[resland] Howe. 21 vols. London: Dent, 1930–34.
House	House, Humphry. *Coleridge: The Clark Lectures 1951–52*. London: Rupert Hart-Davis, 1953.
LB	*Lyrical Ballads*. Ed. R[aymond] L[aurence] Brett and A[lun] R. Jones. London: Methuen, 1965.
Lowes	Lowes, John Livingston. *The Road to Xanadu*. Rev. ed. Boston: Houghton Mifflin, 1930.
LR	*Literary Remains of Samuel Taylor Coleridge*. Ed. Henry Nelson Coleridge. 4 vols. London: Pickering, 1836.

*For the sake of clarity I have occasionally omitted the critical apparatus used by the editors of the *Letters, Notebooks,* and *Philosophical Lectures*.

LS	*Lay Sermons*. Ed. R[eginald] J[ames] White. *The Collected Works of Samuel Taylor Coleridge*. Vol 6. Princeton: Princeton Univ. Press, 1972.
McFarland	McFarland, Thomas. *Coleridge and the Pantheist Tradition*. Oxford: Clarendon Press, 1969.
MC	*Coleridge's Miscellaneous Criticism*. Ed. Thomas M. Raysor. London: Constable, 1936.
*NB**	*The Notebooks of Samuel Taylor Coleridge*. Ed. Kathleen Coburn. 2 vols. New York: Pantheon, 1957–61.
*PL**	*The Philosophical Lectures of Samuel Taylor Coleridge*. Ed. Kathleen Coburn. London: Pilot, 1949.
Prelude	Wordsworth, William. *The Prelude: Or, Growth of a Poet's Mind*. Ed. Ernest de Selincourt and Helen Darbishire. 2nd ed. Oxford: Clarendon Press, 1959.
PW	*The Complete Poetical Works of Samuel Taylor Coleridge*. Ed. Ernest Hartley Coleridge. 2 vols. Oxford, Clarendon Press, 1912. Unless otherwise noted, all references to Coleridge's poetry are to this edition.
SC	*Coleridge's Shakespearean Criticism*. Ed. Thomas M. Raysor. 2 vols. Cambridge, Mass.: Harvard Univ. Press, 1930.
Schneider	Schneider, Elisabeth. *Coleridge, Opium and "Kubla Khan."* Chicago: Univ. of Chicago Press, 1953.
Schulz	Schulz, Max F. *The Poetic Voices of Coleridge: A Study of His Desire for Spontaneity and Passion for Order*. Detroit: Wayne State Univ. Press, 1964.
Warren	Warren, Robert Penn. "A Poem of Pure Imagination: An Experiment in Reading." In Coleridge, *The Rime of the Ancient Mariner*. New York: Reynal and Hitchcock, 1946. Rpt. in *Selected Essays*. New York: Random House, 1958.
Works	*The Complete Works of Samuel Taylor Coleridge*. Ed. W[illiam] G[reenough] T[hayer] Shedd. 7 vols. New York: Harper, 1860.
WPW	*The Poetical Works of William Wordsworth*. Ed. Ernest de Selincourt and Helen Darbishire. 2nd ed. 5 vols. Oxford: Clarendon Press, 1952–59.

Journals

BNYPL	*Bulletin of the New York Public Library*
CE	*College English*
EIC	*Essays in Criticism*
E&S	*Essays and Studies*
JAAC	*Journal of Aesthetics and Art Criticism*
JEGP	*Journal of English and Germanic Philology*
JHI	*Journal of the History of Ideas*
PMLA	*Publications of the Modern Language Association*
REL	*Review of English Literature*
RES	*Review of English Studies*
SIR	*Studies in Romanticism*
SP	*Studies in Philology*

Coleridge's Nightmare Poetry

Chapter I

The Breeze, the Harp, and the Mind

Of all his early poems, Coleridge most admired "The Eolian Harp," the "favorite of *my* poems" as he called it in 1796 (*CL,* I, 295). Although it was first entitled "Effusion XXXV," the poem as it appeared in various editions was not merely a spontaneous record of his feelings of August 20, 1795, the date which Coleridge affixed to the title upon its first publication. The several versions were tentative approaches toward a synthesis of feeling and thought which, because they were embodied in the troublesome symbol of the harp, eluded him. His revisions demonstrate that he was never satisfied with the manner in which he conceived of the relationship between the "I" and the "intellectual Breeze." Ever wary of the moral dangers in the idea of an irresistible external force, yet unwilling to surrender the confidence in the grounds of his being that it gave him, he deleted and inserted lines until, in the final text, he seems to have reached a position where the difficulties were not solved, but where he realized that the problem was unsolvable.

In the 1796 version in *Poems on Various Subjects,*[1] "Effusion XXXV" falls into two roughly parallel sections and a final repudiation. Each of the first two sections begins with Coleridge in a passive state, and each builds its feeling from an analogy with the breeze and the harp. In the first twenty-five lines the breeze is to the harp what the lover is to the "coy Maid"; in the second section the "intellectual Breeze" is to the mind what the natural breeze is to the harp. The subject of the first is love, and of the second, the omnipresence of the "intellectual Breeze" that creates universal harmony.

Coleridge first tries to find in Sara a sympathy and love for which the harp is the symbol. They are sitting beside their cottage at evening gazing on "the star of eve/Serenely brilliant" (ll. 7–8), Hesperus, commonly the planet Venus, and equated somewhat uneasily in Coleridge's mind with wisdom. The reference to myrtle reinforces the connection with Venus, because the myrtle tree was sacred to the goddess, and in earliest days there was a myrtle grove near

[1] Unless otherwise noted line references are to "Effusion XXXV" in *Poems on Various Subjects* (1796), which is reprinted in the Appendix.

her sanctuary in Rome. The spot is thus an appropriate one in which to write a love poem that Coleridge hopes will establish love's innocence. But as the poem progresses, as the implications of the harp symbol reveal themselves, he ironically discovers, not innocence, but his own feelings of guilt.

In the hush of evening the harp placed in the window becomes an image of sexual union. The harp is

> by the desultory breeze caress'd,
> Like some coy Maid half-yielding to her Lover,
> It pours such sweet upbraidings, as must needs
> Tempt to repeat the wrong!
>
> [ll. 14–17]

Stimulated by the response of the harp, the wind increases, and "the long sequacious notes/ Over delicious surges sink and rise" (ll. 18–19). Coleridge fancies that the products of the harp and the breeze are the tunes of "twilight Elfins," thus masking the explicit sexuality of the previous lines. There is no hint here of the metaphysics of the One Life inserted later in this section.

Coleridge becomes aware of the problems in the symbol of the harp in the second section. Previously the breeze had been emblematic of love, but now it becomes the "intellectual Breeze." He imagines that he has ascended a hill alone where he dreams of peace and sees the diamondlike reflections of the sun on the ocean. Images and thoughts flow through his "indolent and passive brain / As wild and various, as the random gales / That swell or flutter on this subject Lute!" (ll. 33–35). Unwilling yet to acknowledge the moral dangers in his phantasies and perhaps not even aware of them, he asks:

> And what if all of animated nature
> Be but organic Harps diversly fram'd,
> That tremble into thought, as o'er them sweeps,
> Plastic and vast, one intellectual Breeze,
> At once the Soul of each, and God of all?
>
> [ll. 36–40]

But no sooner are these words out than he rejects them as "shapings of the unregenerate mind" (l. 47). The obvious problem is that if the mind is like an aeolian harp, it is completely passive, and its products do not depend upon the active powers of the mind itself. When he was composing the *Biographia,* he recalled that earlier he had been unable to "reconcile personality with infinity; and my head was with Spinoza, though my whole heart remained with Paul and John."[2]

[2] *BL,* I, 134. Thomas McFarland interprets the "intellectual Breeze" as "Neoplatonic Spinozism" (p. 166) in his study of Coleridge's struggle with pantheism.

The implications of the "intellectual Breeze" for the problem of his self-knowledge are explicit in a variant of the 1797 text. "All of animated Life" will be played upon by the breeze which produces

Murmurs indistinct and Bursts sublime,
Shrill Discords and most soothing Melodies,
Harmonious from Creation's vast concent—
Thus *God* would be the universal Soul,
Mechaniz'd matter as th'organic harps
And each one's Tunes be that, which each calls I.
[*PW*, II, 1022–23]

If the soul, the "I," is like a tune, then the mind as it appears in the poem has no control over itself. The tune is "wild," "various," and "random." Coleridge recognized that the theology was heretical because the "I" would be irrationally and capriciously constructed. Furthermore, there is the hint that he was afraid that in his own case his speculations on the "I" might be true, that his self was merely an indefinite collection of random notes, unpredictable, unconnected, and without a unifying consciousness. Humphry House is close to the truth when he says that "it may be a moral suspicion of these uncurbed and unruddered associations" that forces Coleridge's repudiation.[3] The fear is not only that his speculations are wrong and morally suspect, but also that uncontrolled associations may be the first indications of a fatal weakness in the self. In the *Biographia* Coleridge wrote that some of Hartley's followers considered the consciousness "as a *result,* as a *tune,* the common product of the breeze and the harp." There he dismisses the idea as an absurdity, for to Hartley's followers "the soul is present only to be pinched or *stroked,* while the very squeals or purring are produced by an agency wholly independent and alien" (*BL,* I, 81).

Jonathan Wordsworth points out that Coleridge was "trying to answer the question which had worried Priestley, as to how far an individual could be at once activated by God, and distinct from him."[4] Coleridge was also attempting to liberate the symbol of the harp from the pantheistic implications that were as destructive to his idea of God as they were to his ideas of individuality. Toward the end of March 1796, at the time he was preparing the final copy for *Poems on Various Subjects,* which was published a few weeks later, he wrote to the Reverend John Edwards: "How is it that Dr Priestley is not an atheist?—He asserts in three different Places, that God not only *does,* but *is,* every thing.—But if God *be* every Thing, every Thing

[3] House, p. 77. See also a somewhat similar analysis in James Boulger's "Imagination and Speculation in Coleridge's Conversation Poems," *JEGP,* 64 (1965), 691–711.

[4] Jonathan Wordsworth, *The Music of Humanity* (London: Nelson, 1969), p. 191.

is God—: which is all, the Atheists assert—. An eating, drinking, lustful *God*—with no *unity* of *Consciousness*. . . ." In consequence of these inferences Coleridge asked, "Has not Dr Priestley forgotten that *Incomprehensibility* is as necessary an attribute of the First Cause?" (*CL*, I, 192–93).

For the later editions of the poem, Coleridge found a less obviously problematic phrase to salvage the symbol of the harp: "the one Life within us and abroad, / Which meets all motion and becomes its soul." Added as they are in the Errata of *Sibylline Leaves,* these words were inserted at approximately the same time or were written after the criticism of the harp image in the *Biographia.* The shift to an emphasis upon the active soul appears to modify the passivity of the harp. Perhaps the addition of the phrase was sufficient for the moment to overcome Coleridge's distrust of the symbol, but there still remains the troublesome presence of the "idle flitting phantasies." Whether they are considered as the product of the breeze from without, or whether they are produced by the active agency of the mind itself, they are an indication of the mind's weakness, and his rejection of these phantasies applies as well to the One Life.

Each section of "Effusion XXXV" leads, not to innocent love and wisdom, but to the rejection of a symbol that embodies his fondest desires. Sara, whom Coleridge tried to unify with the breeze and the current of love, dissociates herself from the symbol elaborated in the second movement. She reproves his pride, recommending instead a hearthside humility. Since she herself has not the immediate experience of the symbol, she fails to understand that it is not a creation of Coleridge's proud speculation. Coleridge himself rejects the harp for other reasons, not because it represents a proud self-assertion or intellectual theorizing devoid of feeling, but because it represents a mind that creates insubstantial phantasies, "Bubbles that glitter as they rise and break / On vain Philosophy's aye-babbling spring" (ll. 48–49). From the knowledge that the mind's creations are these bubbles, he concludes that he is a "sinful and most miserable man / Wilder'd and dark" (ll. 54–55), who can speak innocently of God only as the "Incomprehensible." The structured poetic experience is doubly undermined: Coleridge himself finds unwanted implications in the symbol, and he cannot step toward a truth by perceiving through Sara's alien eyes. Since she does not see as he does, she blocks his further progress and forces him to substitute faith for the intellectually exciting hypothesis that nature is animated by the breeze.

Coleridge's quest, which begins in "Effusion XXXV," can be called a search for a substantial, unified self. "All our Thoughts," he wrote in a notebook in 1807, "all that we abstract from our consciousness & so form the Phaenomenon Self is a Shadow, its whole Substance is the dim yet powerful sense that it is but a Shadow, & ought to belong to a Substance" (*NB*, II, 3026). His meditations on the goal of the quest were most frequent after the publication of his greatest poetry and when he was severely depressed by his failure to reach the goal. The definition of the goal became clearer when he was farthest from it, but the basic problem confronting him was explicit in "Effusion XXXV." The goal of a properly individuated self, he came to learn, could be attained only with the realization of its two aspects: first, the assurance that the self is grounded in a reality outside the self, a reality that can be embodied in objective symbols in nature and, more importantly, in other persons; and second, an active will that unifies the conscious and unconscious, the past and the present, and individuates the self from the undifferentiated oneness of either the One Life or the unconscious.[5]

The first part of his goal is most clearly conveyed in his meditations upon love relationships. Kathleen Coburn has noted that he often attempted "to describe his own consciousness of his need to feel himself as real, and to be reassured of his own identity by means of objects, including love-objects and symbols" (*NB*, II, 3026n). The picture of Coleridge as a transcendentalist who delighted in carrying his speculations on the nature of the self into the realm of Platonic ideas obscures his deep need for a ballast in the empirical world. Whenever he penetrates beyond the bounds of the sensory, whenever he crosses the line between immediate sensation and the world in which there are no anchors in sense, he often retreats, frequently in fear, because his imagination represents the ideal world as insubstantial.

He tried to find in the women he loved an embodiment of an external reality, the One Life that is an active love. His marriage to Sara Fricker in 1795, undertaken as an act of duty because he feared he could not withdraw from it gracefully, enjoyed a few months of happiness, endured a few years of tranquillity, and finally ended in separation some years after he met Sara Hutchinson (Asra)[6] in October 1799. He thought his wife to be totally lacking in sympathy

[5] J[oseph] A[lbert] Appleyard traces the development of Coleridge's philosophical ideas of literature and says that in the first decade of the nineteenth century "Coleridge was working toward a notion of substance that would satisfy the requirements of the individuality of the self while still providing for a universality of essence, and that would explain how created individuals participate in the divine being without necessitating a pantheistic monism" (*Coleridge's Philosophy of Literature* [Cambridge, Mass.: Harvard Univ. Press, 1965], p. 102).

[6] Following George Whalley (*Asra Poems*) and others, I will refer to Sara Hutchinson as Asra, Coleridge's favorite name for her, to distinguish her from his wife and daughter, both of whom were named Sara.

for him and his work (although it is doubtful that this influenced her role in "Effusion XXXV"), and Asra, who was a sister of Wordsworth's wife, could be not merely a lover, but also a symbol of the sympathy granted to him by William and Dorothy Wordsworth and Mary Hutchinson. In November 1803 he confessed privately in his notebook that "my nature requires another Nature for its support" and hoped that his and Asra's souls would be "the same Soul diversely incarnate" (*NB,* I, 1679). Four years later, in the meditation that begins with the realization that the phenomenal self must find its substance, he wrote that the substantial self "can have no marks, no discriminating Characters, no hic est, ille non est / it is simple Substance." Consequently "the craving of True Love" is the longing to find a symbol of the self in another: "Love a sense of Substance / Being seeking to be self-conscious, 1. of itself in a Symbol. 2. of the Symbol as not being itself. 3. of the Symbol as being nothing but in relation to itself" (*NB,* II, 3026). Later in the same year he pondered the kind of support that he required: "It must be one who is & who is not myself . . . Self in me derives its sense of Being from having this one absolute Object, including all others that but for it would be thoughts, notions, irrelevant fancies—yea, my own Self would be—utterly deprived of all connection with her—only more than a thought, because it would be a Burthen—a haunting of the daemon, Suicide" (*NB,* II, 3148). Without a sympathetic lover, Coleridge felt that all his thoughts would exist in a vacuum, and that their existing in a vacuum would be a death. The ability to see oneself in another frees the mind from the prison of subjectivity and keeps alive the soul's "*outness,* its *self-oblivion* united with *Self-warmth*" (*NB,* II, 2540).

The word *outness,* to which Coleridge attaches particular value, was used in this sense by Berkeley in *An Essay towards a New Theory of Vision* (1709). Berkeley argues that the eye, unaided by any other sense, cannot perceive magnitude or distance, which he calls "outness," and that "all visible things are equally in the mind, and take up no part of the external space."[7] This is the familiar doctrine that is fully developed in the *Principles of Human Knowledge* (1710), but the *New Theory of Vision* did not contain the thesis that the sensations of

[7]Berkeley, I, 216. Coleridge's friend and patron Thomas Wedgwood was interested in Berkeley's theories of vision and prepared notes toward a refutation of some of Berkeley's ideas. His thoughts were published posthumously under the title "An Enquiry into the Origin of Our Notion of Distance," *Journal of Science and the Arts Edited at the Royal Institution of Great Britain,* 3 (1817), 1–12. In January 1798 Coleridge told Hazlitt that he admired the *New Theory of Vision* as a "masterpiece of analytical reasoning" (Hazlitt, XVII, 113).

touch are also in the mind. Distance and magnitude are perceived by the sense of touch, not by vision, and the mind, from the constant conjunction of the ideas of touch with the correspondent visual impressions, forms a judgment of distance. Coleridge alludes to these ideas when he speaks of the correspondence between a physical presence and an imaginative conception existing in the mind. In 1805 he explained that his fear of the phantom of subjectivity originated in a "madness from an incapability of hoping that I should be able to marry Mary Evans (and this strange passion of fervent tho' wholly imaginative and imaginary Love uncombinable by my utmost efforts with any regular Hope—/possibly from deficiency of bodily feeling, of tactual ideas connected with the image)." At the end of this note he added, "Important metaphysical Hint the influence of bodily vigor and strong Grasp of Touch in facilitating the passion of Hope...."[8]

The personal hopes and disappointments that he so carefully analyzed in the privacy of his notebooks gave rise to generalizations about the possibility of knowledge of the self. Union with an external reality would provide him with a symbol that revealed the ground of his being and the assurance of a sympathetic response from a community beyond himself. But the danger in undertaking such a quest is that whenever he is unable to find a symbol by which and in which the self can know itself, one that possesses the proper outness, the quest fails. All that remains is the phenomenal self, which Coleridge knew was a mere shadow.

However the definition of an external reality clarified the first part of the goal, it could not be attained without an active will that individuates the self, the second and equally important part of that definition. His revisions of "Effusion XXXV" indicate that he was unable to solve this problem. The danger was that if the self is determined by an exterior force, it has little control over itself and little responsibility for its own construction. Under such conditions the mind submits, abdicating its sovereignity over the self: "Arbitrium = ego, et *agens,* not Voluntas = modificatio mei per alterum, et passio ...," which Coburn translates as "Will is myself *acting,* not [the same as] Choice [which] is a modification of myself by something else, and so a submission... " (*NB*, II, 2439, 2439n). "My will & *I* seem

[8] *NB*, II, 2398. This idea was repeated in the *Philosophical Lectures:* "The first education which we receive, that from our mothers, is given to us by touch; the whole of its process is nothing more than, to express myself boldly, an extended touch by promise. The sense itself, the sense of vision itself, is only acquired by a continued recollection of touch. No wonder therefore, that beginning in the animal state, we should carry this onward through the whole of our being however remote it may be from the true purpose of it" (*PL*, p. 115).

perfect Synonimes," he wrote in an 1803 notebook entry criticizing Kant, "whatever does not apply to the first, I refuse to the latter/ —Any thing strictly of outward Force I refuse to acknowledge, as done *by* me / it is done *with* me . . ." (*NB,* I, 1717). Only with a free will is the achievement of the goal possible; and only when philosophy begins with an act of self-consciousness rather than with the notion of a static substance is the One Life of love perceived as being something other than an inexplicable phantasmagoria.[9]

Another and more public utterance than those in the notebooks, a letter Coleridge wrote to Thomas Clarkson in response to several questions, deals with the problem of self-consciousness. Coleridge answers the query "What is (that is, what can we congruously conceive of) the Soul?" by saying that there is a "growth of consciousness—or the image of that incommunicable attribute of self-comprehension," which is possessed by all creatures who have what he calls "reflex consciousness." This reflex consciousness is a "divine working in us to bind the Past and Future with the Present, and thereby to let in upon us some faint glimmering of that State in which Past, Present, and Future are co-adunated in the adorable I AM" (*CL,* II, 1196–97). Without the "I AM," the ultimate act of self-comprehension, Coleridge declares in *The Statesman's Manual,* "all modes of existence in the external world would flit before us as colored shadows, with no greater depth, root, or fixture, than the image of a rock hath in a gliding stream or the rain-bow on a fast-sailing rain-storm."[10] These images have their origin in Coleridge's poetry: the image of the insubstantial reflection in a stream in "Kubla Khan" and "The Picture," and that of the rainbow on a fast-moving cloud in "Constancy to an Ideal Object"—both alike suggesting that between the search and the fulfillment falls the drifting phenomenal self.

Much later in life in a warm complimentary letter to Charles Aders about Aders's wife, Coleridge repeated the idea he offered to Clarkson, that an individual must seek an awareness of his own continuity:

> It is a maxim with me, to make Life as continuous as possible, by linking on the Present to the Past: and I believe that a large portion of the ingratitude, inconstancy, frivolity, and restless self-weariness so many examples

[9] Coleridge credited Fichte, whose "egoismus" he burlesqued, with beginning philosophy with "an *act,* instead of a *thing* or *substance*" (*BL,* I, 101).

[10] *LS,* p. 78. See also *Friend,* I, 519–20: "But here it behoves us to bear in mind, that all true reality has both its ground and its evidence in the *will,* without which as its complement science itself is but an elaborate game of shadows, begins in abstractions and ends in perplexity."

of which obtrude themselves on every man of observation and reflective habits, is attributable to the *friable,* incohesive sort of existence that characterizes the mere man of the World, a fractional Life made up of successive moments, that neither blend nor modify each other—a life that is strictly symbolized in the thread of Sand thro' the orifice of the Hour-glass, in which the sequence of Grains only *counterfeits* a continuity, and appears a *line* only because the interspaces between the Points are too small to be sensible. Without Memory there can be no hope—the Present is a phantom known only by it's pining, if it do not breathe the vital air of the Future: and what is the Future, but the Image of the Past projected on the mist of the Unknown, and seen with a glory round it's head. But where shall we find the Eternal, which gives the Three in One, and makes all exist in each?[11]

The predictable answer Coleridge gives to his own question is love. But as in previous instances the positive definition of self seems to arise from an experience of the negative, here the repeated image from "Constancy to an Ideal Object," in which a woodsman pursues his own image projected on a cloud.

Coleridge's best-known description of the mind's unity is the famous quotation from Chapter XIV of the *Biographia:* the poet "brings the whole soul of man into activity, with the subordination of its faculties to each other, according to their relative worth and dignity. He diffuses a tone and spirit of unity, that blends, and (as it were) *fuses,* each into each, by that synthetic and magical power, to which we have exclusively appropriated the name of imagination." Significantly, he followed this definition with the assertion that the imagination is "first put in action by the will and understanding, and retained under their irremissive, though gentle and unnoticed, controul" (*BL,* II, 12).

These various thoughts on the nature of the self followed upon Coleridge's first use of the symbol of the harp and were probably a result of the implications of that symbol. They led him toward a theoretical definition of the self. The free will is the only proper means by which the self can be individuated from the phantasmagoria of the

[11] *CL,* V, 266. Coleridge also used the idea in *The Friend,* I, 40: "Every parent possesses the opportunity of observing, how deeply children resent the injury of a delusion; and if men laugh at the falsehoods that were imposed on themselves during their childhood, it is because they are not good and wise enough to contemplate the past in the present, and so to produce by a virtuous and thoughtful sensibility that continuity in their self-consciousness, which Nature has made the law of their animal life." Those who cannot see their own continuity "exist in fragments. Annihilated as to the Past, they are dead to the Future, or seek for the proofs of it everywhere, only not (where alone they can be found) in themselves. A contemporary Poet has exprest and illustrated this sentiment with equal fineness of thought and tenderness of feeling." Coleridge then prints Wordsworth's "My Heart Leaps Up." See also *BL,* I, 59.

unconsciousness and, more importantly, the only way in which the self can imitate God's ultimate act of self-consciousness and thus partake of divine reality.

The syntactic ambiguity of the lines added to "The Eolian Harp" in 1817, "O! the one Life within us and abroad, / Which meets all motion and becomes its soul," permits no distinction between the activity within and without. Is it the action from without which becomes that of the soul, or does that within become the motion of that which is abroad? The pantheistic implications, of which Coleridge was always wary, are still present, and this description of the One Life should be contrasted to his definition of the imagination in Chapter VII of the *Biographia*. He says that his example of the water insect moving up the stream is "no unapt emblem of the mind's self-experience in the act of thinking": "the little animal *wins* its way up against the stream, by alternate pulses of active and passive motion, now resisting the current, and now yielding to it in order to gather strength and a momentary *fulcrum* for a further propulsion" (*BL,* I, 85–86). He calls the faculty that is both active and passive the imagination. In its active phase it resists the motion of the stream; it is passive only to gain strength to resist again. The motion of the insect is not the stream's, but in the lines on the One Life added in 1817 the mind's motion is identical to that from without. Defined by the example of the insect, the mind is an independent entity preserving its individuality, and the pantheism is purged. The added lines do not, therefore, present a complete solution to the problems inherent in the symbol of the harp. By the time Coleridge added them he recognized the necessity of separating his imagination from that force he had called the One Life.

Elsewhere in Coleridge the idea of the One Life is fitted out to conform with the more orthodox requirements of his theology. As merely the "plastic immaterial Nature" (*CL,* I, 294) that does not possess the essential unity of consciousness, it obscures his need for a personal God. The idea reappears in *The Statesman's Manual,* where he is careful to preserve the individuality of each within the definition of the whole: "In the Bible every agent appears and acts as a self-subsisting individual: each has a life of its own, and yet all are one Life."[12] On the other hand, when the idea of an irresistible external force is dis-

[12] *LS,* p. 31. The earliest Coleridgean use of this phrase that I have found occurs in 1802 and also emphasizes the individuality of each: Coleridge thought "that every Thing has a Life of its own, & that we are all *one Life*" (*CL,* II, 864). Wordsworth used the phrase in Book II of the 1805 *Prelude:* "for in all things / I saw one life, and felt that it was joy" (ll. 429–30), probably written before October 1800 (*Prelude,* p. xlvii).

tinguished from that of a personal God, it undergoes a strange transformation into a threatening, uncontrolled flow of association. While the idea of the One Life is altered explicitly in his philosophic prose, the second transformation is implicit in his poetry. When the second takes place and when the threat formerly thought to come from without is more accurately understood as coming from within, nature and the external world disappear as significant dimensions in Coleridge's poetic landscape. The despair of "Dejection: an Ode" and the use of the harp in that poem are occasioned by the separation of the self from a joyous participation in significant relationships with nature and with other minds and by an acknowledgement that all that is left to him is the residue of a once attractive idea.

Coleridge's use of faculty psychology to explain the mind is both embarrassing to modern readers, who may prefer to talk of a *gestalt,* and awkward for Coleridge himself, who sought to speak of the mind as a single unified organism. Perhaps it was true that he did not have the proper terms to say what he wanted to say about the mind, and his bizarre toying with etymology offers further proof that he found his language inadequate. While his use of faculty psychology caused some problems in his effort to define a unified mind, it gave a rather accurate picture of the fragmentation of his own self as he observed it. Contemporaneous with his notebook entries and letters that reveal his aspirations for the establishment of his individual self are those that expose his frequent failure to attain any experience of himself as a fully integrated being. The frustration of his love for Asra is only symptomatic of a larger failure to find for himself symbols of a reality exterior to himself. Coincident with a diminished sense of an exterior reality is the powerlessness to assert that essential act of consciousness which is the self. The result of these failures was a disintegration of personality that he recognized as a death, or, in moments when he was able to make a moral judgment upon himself, a suicide. He was both an actor in his own tragedy and the critic who observed and analyzed the motivations of the actor. His diagnosis of his own afflictions opened new fields of insight into psychology and pointed to new paths of literary criticism. At the same time, however, it pointed to a sharp division of his personality, because he began to regard the actor as someone separate from him for whom he was not responsible.

When Coleridge describes a faculty working split off from the others and without reference to them, it is usually presented as resulting in death or madness. Often his comments on the deadening influence of a complete reliance upon the understanding, the faculty which deals only with phenomena, are contained in his polemics against the mechanists of his and earlier ages, whose philosophy he deplored. The "products of the mere *reflective* faculty partook of DEATH, and were as the rattling twigs and sprays in winter, into which a sap was yet to be propelled from some root to which I had not penetrated" (*BL,* I, 98). His rhetoric upholds the claims of a vitalist philosophy, yet one cannot fully explain the vigor of his rhetoric by an imaginary rekindling of the arguments in which he was engaged. His participation in these debates was never disinterested; most of his contributions were derived from his own self-watching mind, and the moral urgency that is the rhetoric of his position was generated from knowledge of his own pain.

Of yet more relevance for a reading of his poetry than his insistence upon the limitations of the understanding are his differing ways of distinguishing between fancy and imagination, one of which was to draw a parallel distinction between delirium and mania. The distinction between fancy and imagination "is no less grounded in nature, than that of delirium from mania, or Otway's

> 'Lutes, lobsters, seas of milk, and ships of amber,'

from Shakespeare's

> 'What! have his daughters brought him to this pass?'

or from the preceding apostrophe to the elements" (*BL,* I, 62). Both Belvidera in *Venice Preserved* and Lear, whose address to the elements precedes his question about Edgar, suffer from kinds of madness. The association of fancy and imagination with aberrant states of consciousness remained with Coleridge until the final year of his life: "You may conceive the difference in kind between the Fancy and the Imagination in this way,—that if the check of the senses and the reason were withdrawn, the first would become delirium, and the last mania."[13] He was more familiar with the fancy and imagination without these checks.

Fancy, defined in the *Biographia,* is "Memory emancipated from the order of time and space" and "modified by that empirical phenomenon of the will, which we express by the word CHOICE," by which Coleridge implies a submission to an external force.[14] Elsewhere he explains that the function of fancy is to create an outward form for the mind's conceptions, to provide the mind's creations with the necessary objectivity. The mere form, or body, is necessarily a dead thing by means of which life can be understood, but which is not itself alive. Fancy is the "Gorgon Head, which *looked* death into

[13] *Table Talk,* June 23, 1834, in *Works,* VI, 517–18.
[14] *BL,* I, 202. See *NB,* II, 2439, quoted above p. 7.

every thing." The error, he explains, lies "not in the faculty itself, without which there would be no *fixation*, consequently, no distinct perception or conception, but in the gross idolatry of those who abuse it, & make that the goal & end which should be only a means of arriving at it."[15]

As he was quick to discover, the imagination, like the fancy, could become diseased by operating by itself without this "check of the senses and the reason." The result is a mania in which, as Crabb Robinson reported from Coleridge's conversation, "the imagination under excitement generates and produces a form of its own,"[16] a form which possesses a reality only in the mind. In a letter of 1802 he confessed that "from an unhealthy & reverie-like vividness of *Thoughts*" and an exclusion of impressions from without, his ideas and wishes were "to a diseased degree disconnected from *motion* & *action.*" Realizing that his reveries were signs of a diseased will, he further confessed that "'I will' & 'I will not' are phrases, both of them equally, of rare occurrence in my dictionary" (*CL,* II, 782–83). He tried to maintain a correspondence between the activity of the mind and the impressions from without. Too great a reliance upon his own dream creation drove him into mania and isolation; too frequent an abdication of his own will produced delirium, a form of madness equally self-destructive.

Coleridge was cautious of considering the imagination as a faculty that could by itself create truth. The imagination that creates the whole man is governed by reason. In an outline for his projected poem "The Soother of Absence" he wrote, "Mix up Truth & Imagination, so that the Imag. may spread its own indefiniteness over that which really happened, & Reality its sense of substance & distinctness to Imagination" (*NB,* I, 1541). After the plans for the pantisocratic community failed, he explained his youthful enthusiasm for the project. He had first formed an intuition of what he thought society ought to be like and then tried to project his intuition upon actual conditions. As he was to learn, the plan was utterly impractical, but nevertheless he had tried to "make ideas & realities stand side by side, the one as vivid as the other" (*CL,* II, 1000). These two apparently insignificant notes contain important clues to his methods of

[15] Notebook 17, quoted by Kathleen Coburn, "Reflections in a Coleridge Mirror: Some Images in His Poems," in *From Sensibility to Romanticism,* ed. Frederick W. Hilles and Harold Bloom (New York: Oxford, 1965), p. 419. The entry was probably written between June 1810 and April 1811.

[16] *Diary, Reminiscences, and Correspondence of Henry Crabb Robinson,* ed. Thomas Sadler (London: Macmillan, 1872), I, 160. The note was entered in Robinson's Diary for Nov. 15, 1810.

thinking in general. To illustrate a similar point, George Whalley selectes a passage from the *Philosophical Lectures:*

Plato began in meditation, thought deeply within himself of the goings-on of his own mind and of the powers that there were in that mind, conceived to himself how this could be, and if it were, what must be the necessary results and agencies of it, and then looked abroad to ask if this were a dream, or whether it were indeed a revelation from within, and a waking reality. He employed his observation as the interpreter of his meditation, equally free from the fanatic who abandons himself to the wild workings of the magic cauldron of his own brain mistaking every form of delirium for reality, and from the cold sensualist who looks at death as the alone real, or life of the world, by not considering that the very object was seen to him only by the seeing powers, and what a little further consideration would have led him to deduce, that that which could make him see it must be an agent, and a power like his own, whilst that which was merely seen, which was purely passive, could have no other existence than what arose out of an active power that had produced it.[17]

The characteristic movement from imaginative conception to the search for its verification is analogous to Coleridge's search for the self. In both cases the goal is a significant objective symbolism, and this movement informs the Conversation Poems, where he typically begins with an imaginative ideal and attempts to verify it by direct observation.

During the conversation with Crabb Robinson, Coleridge illustrated the disease of the imagination by relating an incident which, in his notebook, he called a "pretty optical fact" (*NB,* I, 1668). Climbing in the mountains of the Lake Country, he watched a kite soaring in the sky. Suddenly he turned his head in another direction and saw two more kites about the same distance from him and gazed at them for some moments until he realized that he had never before seen two kites together. Not until he wondered at the unusual presence of the two birds did he realize that they were not birds at all but the last leaves hanging on the branches of a young fruit tree. He was so intent upon watching the original kite that when he switched his attention to the leaves, his mind and feelings were still concentrating on the bird, and the intensity of the original perception distorted his perception of the dangling leaves. Only when the intellect informed him that he had never seen two kites together was he able to restore "the check of the senses." This event appears to be a trivial one, but Coleridge, who never let the larger importance of any interesting

[17] *PL,* p. 186, quoted by George Whalley in "On Reading Coleridge," in *S. T. Coleridge,* ed. R. L. Brett (London: Bell, 1971), p. 5.

phenomenon of this sort escape him, carefully wrote down all of the details of this experience in his notebook and later used it as an instance of a diseased imagination.

He explained to Southey in 1803 that he had finally grasped the "whole mystery of frightful Dreams, & Hypocondriacal Delusions." He used the somewhat inadequate example of a live coal's being whirled in a circle and the mind's seeing not the separate successive points of light but a completed circle. If one supposes that the circle of light is produced by the imagination itself rather than by the physical structure of the human eye, he will possess a good idea of the "*aggregation* of slight Feelings by the force of a diseasedly retentive Imagination" (*CL,* II, 974). This account is strikingly similar to the "pretty optical fact" he mentioned in conjunction with the distortion of vision when he saw the kites. In both there is a loss of the distinct impressions and the creation by the active imagination of an idea that has no correlative in sensation; and in this case the loss is accompanied by an intensification of feeling.

As a literary critic Coleridge judged the health of a character by the balance that character was able to maintain between feelings and exterior realities. Hamlet and Lady Macbeth are obvious examples of persons who are unable to control their imaginations and whose actions are determined by the flux of their emotions. One of his most extensive analyses of a diseased imagination is a discussion of Luther in *The Friend.* Luther was, in Coleridge's analysis, "a Poet indeed, as great a Poet as ever lived in any age or country; but his poetic images were so vivid, that they mastered the Poet's own mind! He was *possessed* with them, as with substances distinct from himself." When thoughts dominate the consciousness so often and so vividly, they take on the appearances of substances exterior to the mind. Coleridge observed in 1823 that "terror and the heated imagination will, even in the daytime, create all sorts of features, shapes, and colors, out of a single object, possessing none of them in reality."[18]

While Luther was secluded in the fortress at Wartburg, he had "a brain-image of the Devil, vivid enough to have acquired apparent *Outness.*" Just previous to his seeing the devil, Luther had been busy at his translation of the Hebrew Bible. His concentration was not repaid with any insight, and the illumination he received from the Vulgate further added to his frustration. The Greek text was also of no use to him. His intellect thwarted, he dropped off into a reverie:

> Disappointed, despondent, enraged, ceasing to *think,* yet continuing his brain on the stretch in solicitation of a thought; and gradually giving himself up to

[18] *Works,* VI, 271.

angry fancies, to recollections of past persecutions, to uneasy fears and inward defiances and floating Images of the evil Being, their supposed personal author; he sinks, without perceiving it, into a trance of slumber: during which his brain retains its waking energies, excepting that what would have been mere *thoughts* before, now (the action and counter-weight of his senses and of their impressions being withdrawn) shape and condense themselves into *things,* into realities! Repeatedly half-wakening, and his eye-lids as often reclosing, the objects which really surround him form the place and scenery of his dream. All at once he sees the Arch-fiend coming forth on the wall of the room, from the very spot perhaps, on which his eyes had been fixed vacantly during the perplexed moments of his former meditation: the Ink-stand, which he had at the same time been using, becomes associated with it: and in that struggle of rage, which in these distempered dreams almost constantly precedes the helpless terror by the pain of which we are finally awakened, he *imagines* that he hurls it at the intruder, or not improbably in the first instant of awakening, while yet both his imagination and his eyes are possessed by the dream, he *actually* hurls it.[19]

Again, as so often in other contexts, Coleridge emphasizes the retreat into subjectivity and the intensity of emotion, and the retreat destroys any connection with objective reality. Since the power of the objective reality to control, or at least act as a break upon, the flow of emotions is reduced, the thoughts and images that represent the fears become, or appear to be, substantial realities. These realities, of course, do not embody any universal reality, but they do reflect Luther's detestation of the devil, a creation that he thinks comes from outside himself. The vividness and apparent outness produce terror, for in such a diseased state, one takes them to be the actual conditions of the universe. In 1807 Coleridge wrote in his own cipher system: "Thought becomes a thing when it acts at once on your . . . consciousness . . . therefore I dread to tell my whole & true case. It seems to make a substantial reality / I want it to remain a thought in which I may be deceived wholly."[20]

The final result of his isolation from the "check of the reason and the senses" is the dreary knowledge that he exists in a vacuum, like the mariner "Alone, alone, all, all alone / Alone on a wide wide sea!" His separation from home and friends during his trip to Germany caused him to write to his wife that he had "experienced such an extinction of *Light* in my mind, I have been so forsaken by all the *forms* and *colourings* of Existence, as if the *organs* of Life had been dried up; as if only simple BEING remained, blind and stagnant!" (*CL,* I, 470). A few months later, upon hearing of the death of his second son,

[19] *Friend,* I, 140–42.

[20] *NB,* II, 3045 and 3045n. I have simplified Coburn's transcription.

Berkeley, he admitted that he was paralyzed by "the vacancy that has been made—when no where any thing corresponds to the form which will perhaps for ever dwell on my mind" (*CL,* I, 483). The despair that he felt occasionally while he was writing his best poetry became the habit of his soul after 1802 when his verse is haunted by specters and abstractions whose sole reality is in his mind. His constant tendency to think of himself as an isolated soul and an outcast generated in him a fear of an imagination that could project only objects of fear. Fear without any substantial object is angst.

The best of the Conversation Poems begin with Coleridge's feeling of loss and isolation and move outwards to reestablish a viable connection with nature and with the community of other minds. When he is most successful, as in "This Lime-Tree Bower," he does reach a joyous union with nature through the mediation of other minds. But more often his joy is that of contemplating those who are not subject to the loss and isolation to which he is subject. His delights, vicarious as they are, are nonetheless real to him, even though they do not bring him to the fulfillment of his personal quest.

Chapter II

The Dead Calm of the Conversation Poems

George McLean Harper, who first gave the name "Conversation Poems" to the group of eight Coleridge poems, offered the alternative title of "Poems of Friendship. They cannot be even vaguely understood unless the reader knows what persons Coleridge has in mind."[1] Harper's remark has been almost entirely forgotten, perhaps because the tone of his essay indulges too much his own sentiments. Yet it ought not to be forgotten that these poems are addressed to persons who are neither inert listeners nor merely symbols of Coleridge's own consciousness. They are centers of perception distinct from Coleridge himself. After "Reflections on Having Left a Place of Retirement," Coleridge himself does not directly participate in joy; the Wordsworths, Lamb, and Hartley Coleridge are at the center of the vision in the other Conversation Poems, while Coleridge enters only vicariously into their experiences. Coleridge often assumes, as Walter Jackson Bate so aptly puts it, the role of "benevolent and understanding usher" who directs others to new insights.[2]

Coleridge's complaisance is not merely the mark of his obliging personality; it is rather an attempt to step toward an imaginative understanding of the unity of all minds while at the same time preserving his individuality. In these poems he seems to be approaching poetically the thought he offered in 1806 to Thomas Clarkson, who had asked him, "What is ... the soul?" Coleridge responded that it consisted in a consciousness of "*a* continuousness" in the growth of the soul and added that

> this state & growth of reflex consciousness ... is not conceivable without the action of kindred souls on each other, i.e. the modification of each by each, and of each by the Whole. A male & female Tyger is neither more or less

[1]"Coleridge's Conversation Poems," in *Spirit of Delight* (New York: Holt, 1928); rpt. in *English Romantic Poets,* ed. M. H. Abrams (New York: Oxford, 1960), p. 145. Harper includes in his classification "The Eolian Harp," "Reflections on Having Left a Place of Retirement," "This Lime-Tree Bower My Prison," "Fears in Solitude," "The Nightingale," "Dejection," and "To William Wordsworth." A detailed discussion of "The Eolian Harp" is in chapter 1, and the last two poems I shall discuss in chapter 7.

[2]*Coleridge* (New York: Macmillan, 1968), p. 50.

whether you suppose them only existing in their appropriate wilderness, or whether you suppose a thousand Pairs. But Man is truly altered by the co-existence of other men; his faculties cannot be developed in himself alone, & only by himself. Therefore the human race not by a bold metaphor, but in a sublime reality, approach to, & might become, one body whose Head is Christ (the Logos).

[*CL*, II, 1197]

Probably this conviction was not fully formulated when Coleridge began to write in the conversational mode, but as he matured in the form he realized that his aspirations for his imagination would be achieved insofar as he could establish an identity with the other consciousness in the poem. In "The Eolian Harp" there is an awkward discontinuity between his own speculations and Sara's admonition. He could not integrate her mind into the poem because she herself had not experienced what he had; hers was an entirely different world that had no common basis with his. To overcome this difficulty in later poems, he placed the other mind at the center of imaginative vision. In "This Lime-Tree Bower My Prison" and "Frost at Midnight," Lamb, the Wordsworths, and Hartley participate in joy, and Coleridge reaches toward that vision through their perceptions. A measure of the success of Coleridge's quest is the degree to which he can realize this identification of his consciousness with that of the other mind.

Most modern descriptions of the structure of the Conversation Poems take little account of the presence of other minds. Harper established the commonly accepted account in an observation on "Reflections on Having Left a Place of Retirement": "The poem begins with a quiet description of the surrounding scene and, after a superb flight of imagination, brings the mind back to the starting-point, a pleasing device which we may call the 'return.'"[3] Harper's definition of a "return" implies a circular motion that later commentators have taken as a basis for more detailed studies of the structure of all the poems. Humphry House, for instance, notes that in "Frost at Midnight" the organizing principle is "the 'I'—the seeing, remembering, projecting mind—the man sitting in a cottage room at night. From the room the mind moves out, by stages, first to the physical context of weather and sound, then to the village, then to the world—'all the numberless goings-on of life'. Next with a swift contracting transition, unexplained, in the middle of a line (l. 13) it comes in again to the fire."[4] House implies that there may not be one

[3]Harper, p. 148.
[4]House, pp. 79–80.

but a series of expansions and contractions of the poet's consciousness. Similarly, Albert Gérard has seen in "The Eolian Harp" an ascending movement and "a heart-beat rhythm of systole and diastole, of contraction and expansion, in which the poet's attention is wandering to and fro between his concrete immediate experience and the wide, many-faceted world of the non-self."[5] In substantial agreement with previous critics, Max Schulz observes that the unity of the poems depends upon "a curving pattern of emotion" and "a circular progression of thought" as well as a philosophy of the One Life and an imaginative apprehension of the "totality of experience." He notes that there are not one but two circular motions, two "calm-exaltation-calm parabolas": "In each poem Coleridge starts conversationally in the hushed air of a momentarily silenced earth. Moved by a sudden thought or incident, his mood rises to a climax of exalted philosophical or ethical meditation and then sinks from this impassioned tone through quiet talk to the silence that had reigned in the beginning—only to repeat the sequence again."[6]

The Conversation Poems, however, do not fit the paradigm of strict symmetry that Coleridge himself created.[7] The variations of the paradigm are more significant for a study of Coleridge the poet than the generalizations of the paradigm itself. In the more mature Conversation Poems his mind is at first halted by his inability to move outwards toward nature. Thomas Poole's garden is at first to him a prison in "This Lime-Tree Bower," where he is simply unable to respond to the beauty of the natural world that surrounds him; and especially in "Frost at Midnight" he is unable to penetrate the mystery of the silence. Thus frustrated by his inability to respond to the natural world, he turns to other minds to perceive the natural world through them and at the same time to assure himself that he is a portion of a vital life constituted by other minds. Only in "This Lime-Tree Bower" is there a complete unity of the actual sensations and Coleridge's imaginative re-creations of them. Later, in "Frost at Midnight," there is a sharp distinction between his own anxiety about his isolation and Hartley's intuitive knowledge of "that eternal language, which thy God / Utters."

[5]Gérard's observations were first offered in "The Systolic Rhythm: The Structure of Coleridge's Conversation Poems," *EIC,* 10 (1960), 307–19, and were repeated in *English Romantic Poetry* (Berkeley and Los Angeles: Univ. of Calif. Press, 1968), pp. 29–30.

[6]Schulz, p. 82.

[7]For an interesting study of the history of the form and Coleridge's use of it, see M. H. Abrams, "Structure and Style in the Greater Romantic Lyric," in *From Sensibility to Romanticism,* pp. 527–60.

A further difficulty in a strict application of the paradigm is that when there is a discontinuity between the minds in the poem, the "return" is often a retreat from the speculations to which Coleridge seems so emotionally committed and a repudiation that leaves him finally still vexed about his relationship to the universe. The most notable example of a retreat is "The Eolian Harp," in which his acquiescence to Sara's admonitions is not merely the accommodating gesture of a new husband or a docile submission to her ideals of humility. The voice that rejects the speculations is Coleridge's own, not hers, and he rejects the speculations because he finds inconsistencies and undesirable implications in them. "Reflections on Having Left a Place of Retirement" also contains a repudiation, not only of the retirement in the lower paradise of the garden around the cot but also of the imaginative flights that are possible for one so deceptively emparadised. Although the other Conversation Poems do not contain an explicit repudiation of what has gone before, the poet withdraws himself from the center of the stage, where his place is taken by the person to whom the poem is addressed.

Because of its political themes, "Reflections on Having Left a Place of Retirement" seems an anomaly in the group. Much more of a public poem like "Fears in Solitude," to which it is linked by the motto "sermoni propriora," which Coleridge applied to both,[8] it was written on the occasion of his leaving Clevedon late in 1795 to return to Bristol to be nearer the library and his literary and political associates and to publish *The Watchman*. It does, however, follow the pattern set by "The Eolian Harp"; it begins with a quiet scene, moves to a meditation upon the omnipresence of divinity, and then, like the earlier poem, rejects that meditation because Coleridge finds ethical problems in it. Although the moral qualms he feels about reposing in such a spot do not strike as deeply against his metaphysical and emotional needs as those in "The Eolian Harp," they do lead him to deny that retirement is acceptable in turbulent times. Retirement is not as destructive of the self as are the insubstantial phantasies of the harp, but it is a luxury he cannot afford if he is going to join a Christian community. If he is going to join that community he must renounce Clevedon, the particular spot of his retirement symbolized by the myrtle and jasmin in the two poems.

His cottage at Clevedon is a retreat from the world, a refuge where

[8]Coleridge used the phrase as an epigraph for "Reflections," and on a manuscript of "Fears in Solitude" he wrote "N.B. The above is perhaps not Poetry,—but rather a sort of middle thing between Poetry and Oratory—sermoni propriora. —Some parts are, I am conscious, too tame even for animated prose" (*PW*, I, 257).

he can nourish the virtues of modesty, humility, and tranquillity and where he is free from the temptations of the active life. It is not an Eden of complete innocence. The "green and woody" landscape refreshes the eye, and, most importantly, it is the "Valley of Seclusion," more a restriction than a haven for permanent repose. Man's Fall has already occurred, and the Coleridge who lives in the valley has experienced the world's evil and has returned to be refreshed at the humble cottage. Although most likely not the same spot, the dell of "Fears in Solitude" is symbolically equivalent to that in "Reflections on Having Left a Place of Retirement." In "Fears in Solitude" the dell has its profuse blooming flowers and its skylark and is loved by

> The humble man, who, in his youthful years,
> Knew just so much of folly, as had made
> His early manhood more securely wise!
> Here he might lie on fern or withered heath,
> While from the singing lark (that sings unseen
> The minstrelsy that solitude loves best),
> And from the sun, and from the breezy air,
> Sweet influences trembled o'er his frame;
> And he, with many feelings, many thoughts,
> Made up a meditative joy, and found
> Religious meanings in the forms of Nature!
>
> [ll. 14–24]

Clevedon has the same effect upon the "wealthy son of Commerce" whose life, presumably, is spent in a mad scramble for "idle gold." Having intruded in the place of retirement, he muses "with wiser feelings" and is calmed. If we are reassured by his being calmed, if our expectations about the strength of the virtues of retirement are satisfied, there is also a disquieting note in the intrusion. The "son of Commerce" is referred to as "Bristowa's citizen." It is difficult to determine exactly how many of the contemporary connotations Coleridge intended for the word *citizen,* but it would be impossible for someone moving in liberal circles, as he did in those years, to ignore its associations with the French Revolution. The "son of Commerce" is humbled by the valley, and yet, too, he is a citizen of the world, one who leads the active life and is not secluded.

After the visit of the citizen and in contrast to it Coleridge mentions the unobtrusive song of the skylark:

> Oft with patient ear
> Long-listening to the viewless sky-lark's note
> (Viewless, or haply for a moment seen
> Gleaming on sunny wings) in whisper'd tones
> I've said to my Belovéd, "Such, sweet Girl!

The inobtrusive song of Happiness,
Unearthly minstrelsy! then only heard
When the Soul seeks to hear; when all is hush'd,
And the Heart listens!"

[ll. 18–26]

The skylark does not spoil the seclusion and quiet; in fact, being infrequently seen, it is a proper hermit to inhabit this valley. Furthermore it is heard only when the heart listens. But only the heart hears the song, and however spiritually enriching, in the context of the rest of the poem, it is also restricting and limiting.

There is an attempt to transcend the "low Dell," to escape seclusion, through intensification of the experiences of the bird's song. The mental elevation of the song is followed by a physical ascent of the hill to see the Bristol Channel. This first effort to leave the valley is made with "perilous toil," and the view that opens to him reinforces his previous calm, love of peace, and knowledge that the natural world is God's temple, all of which fills his heart with joy. At the summit of these private experiences "No *wish* profan'd my overwhelméd heart. / Blest hour! It was a luxury,—to be!" Such a view, desirable for a Coleridge who loved to accommodate his imagination to the vast, is rejected with an acidity that is surprising in these poems. When he is constrained to leave the valley for the active life he asks:

Was it right,
While my unnumber'd brethern toil'd and bled,
That I should dream away the entrusted hours
On rose-leaf beds, pampering the coward heart
With feelings all too delicate for use?

[ll. 44–48]

The toil of climbing the mountain loses all its reward by comparison with the toil of the citizens for mankind, because, as much as the toil for wealth, it is a luxury which Coleridge's moral self cannot afford.

Coleridge wishes nothing more than to imagine himself worshipping in nature's temple, but he has been deceived by the elevating song of the skylark, which must be rejected as dreamlike. The heart is overwhelmed in the Valley of Seclusion, but in the active world he will "join head, heart, and hand, / Active and firm, to fight the bloodless fight / Of Science, Freedom, and the Truth in Christ." One of the reasons for the rejection of the imaginative vision is that it is a selfish indulgence that restricts the activities of all the human faculties. Even the benefactor who grants with a cold, indifferent gesture is superior to

> The sluggard Pity's vision-weaving tribe!
> Who sigh for Wretchedness, yet shun the Wretched,
> Nursing in some delicious solitude
> Their slothful loves and dainty sympathies!
>
> [ll. 56–59]

Finally there is what Harper has called the return of the poem:

> Yet oft when after honourable toil
> Rests the tir'd mind, and waking loves to dream,
> My spirit shall revisit thee, dear Cot!
> Thy Jasmin and thy window-peeping Rose,
> And Myrtles fearless of the mild sea-air.
> And I shall sigh fond wishes—sweet Abode!
> Ah!—had none greater! And that all had such!
> It might be so—but the time is not yet.
> Speed it, O Father! Let thy kingdom come!
>
> [ll. 63–71]

Until the coming of the millennium when the busy commerce of the social world and the quiet valley of retirement will be reconciled, the valley can be only a temporarily refreshing dream which, if taken for the sole reality, can become a valley of sterile and stifling seclusion. And until such time when the millennium arrives, the world remains fallen, and the separate fragments of experience—that of the steady turmoil of Bristol and England and that of the best eighteenth-century retirement—are both false. The reconciliation, the full unity of Clevedon and Bristol, is not in the poem except in the prayer for the coming of the millennium. The burden of being born into the mortal world is being forced to reject those very characteristics of Eden and retirement that form its major delights; paradise must be regained by the rejection of its dreamlike image.

The choice Coleridge is forced to make excludes its alternative. Such, too, is the burden of the fallen world. By choosing to return to Bristol, where he had lectured against the slave trade and against the suspensions of civil liberties, he is forced to ignore his private aspirations. To abdicate his public role would be to dissolve the bonds which tie him to a Christian community. In 1795 it may still have been possible to hope for the establishment of a country of romance, as Wordsworth first saw the France of the Revolution, even though by then the pantisocratic scheme of the Bristol radicals had vanished. The Valley of Seclusion is not pantisocracy, a model for a perfect society, because it is a partial one. Similarly, the view from the Bristol Channel, however much it images God's creation, includes slight signs of human habitation. The city spire is faint.

In these two early Conversation Poems, "The Eolian Harp" and

"Reflections on Having Left a Place of Retirement," two minds or alternatives conflict. The hearth and the hillside in "The Eolian Harp," like Clevedon and Bristol in "Reflections," are not reconciled; the harp symbol is rejected for the humility of his wife, that "Meek Daughter in the Family of Christ," and the secluded valley, for the Christian battle for truth. Coleridge's tendency is to select the alternative that would admit him into a human community of other minds. Where he fails in these two poems, he succeeds later in "This Lime-Tree Bower My Prison," for he is able to establish a personal relationship to sympathetic members of a human community and through their mediation to assert his place in a harmonious universe.

"This Lime-Tree Bower" opens with regret for a loss he has suffered. He had hoped to be able to accompany Lamb and the Wordsworths on their walk over the hills and to accumulate "Beauties and feelings, such as would have been / Most sweet to my remembrance even when age / Had dimm'd mine eyes to blindness," Wordsworthian spots of time that would remain sources of vitality. The emphasis in the opening lines is upon absence, the absence of his friends and the complete vacancy in which he is imprisoned. Poole's garden is not to him a manifestation of nature; it is only a dead spot in which he is locked by his subjectivity and selfhood. His task throughout the poem is to discover a way of overcoming his loss and breaking out of the emptiness of his self, but before he can look directly at nature he must follow Lamb and the Wordsworths in his imagination.

He follows in imagination their walk along the ridge of the Quantock Hills, descending at noon into a ravine, and emerging to survey the sunset. From his recollections, his imagination composes the scenes they see, scenes that are not unmodified random sensations but emblems of his plight and which offer hints toward a solution to the problem of his inability to perceive nature around him. The two scenes permit him to return at the end of the poem to see the natural garden.

The descent from the ridge is the first of these scenes:

> The roaring dell, o'erwooded, narrow, deep,
> And only speckled by the mid-day sun;
> Where its slim trunk the ash from rock to rock
> Flings arching like a bridge;—that branchless ash,
> Unsunn'd and damp, whose few poor yellow leaves
> Ne'er tremble in the gale, yet tremble still,
> Fann'd by the water-fall!
>
> [ll. 10–16]

There is a correspondence between Coleridge himself, isolated in the bower, and the ash that grows by the stream. Like the poet, the ash is isolated from the sun, a source of life for the tree, and the breeze, a source of animation. Inspiration and the benevolent powers of nature, traditionally symbolized by the breeze and the sun, are also absent to Coleridge. Yet the ash is not completely isolated from the forces of nature; it is animated by the rush of water and thus possesses a life in the secluded spot. In the Fenwick note to "Lines Written in Early Spring," Wordsworth describes what must have been the very spot that Coleridge had in mind:

> The brook fell down a sloping rock so as to make a waterfall considerable for that country, and across the pool below had fallen a tree, an ash, if I rightly remember, from which rose perpendicularly boughs in search of the light intercepted by the deep shade above. The boughs bore leaves of green that for want of sunshine had faded into almost lily-white; and from the underside of this natural sylvan bridge depended long and beautiful tresses of ivy which waved gently in the breeze that might poetically speaking be called the breath of the waterfall.
>
> [*WPW*, IV, 411-12]

The images in the "roaring dell" have been transformed into a symbolic landscape. Although immediate sensations are absent, Coleridge has prepared himself to receive nature directly.

The second scene is more obviously related to his own particular imprisonment. Like Coleridge, Lamb has been imprisoned away from nature. The visit liberates him from London and its associations with his mother's tragic death. This affliction of evil is far more real than Coleridge had experienced. Now Lamb

> Struck with deep joy may stand, as I have stood,
> Silent with swimming sense; yea, gazing round
> On the wide landscape, gaze till all doth seem
> Less gross than bodily; and of such hues
> As veil the Almighty Spirit, when yet he makes
> Spirits perceive his presence.
>
> [ll. 38–43]

That the delight attributed to Lamb had also been Coleridge's there can be little doubt. The explicit parallel between Coleridge's imprisonment and Lamb's residence in London suggests so. Additionally, Coleridge included these lines in a letter to John Thelwall to explain his own feelings:

> I can *at times* feel strongly the beauties, you describe, in themselves, & for themselves—but more frequently *all things* appear little—all the knowledge, that can be acquired, child's play—the universe itself—what but an immense

heap of *little* things?—I can contemplate nothing but parts, & parts are all *little*—!—My mind feels as if it ached to behold & know something *great*—something *one* & *indivisible*—and it is only in the faith of this that rocks or waterfalls, mountains or caverns give me the sense of sublimity or majesty! —But in this faith *all things* counterfeit infinity!—"Struck with the deepest calm of Joy" I stand.

[*CL*, I, 349]

All of the beauties of nature appear as little things, as mere objects, fixed and dead, unless they are seen in the light of a conviction that the mind can know something great. Only in this faith, Coleridge says, do the sensations from the objective world have any meaning for him. The faith in the unity of all creation is prior to his appreciation of its particular beauties. And within "This Lime-Tree Bower" the imaginative conception of nature is prior to his appreciation of Poole's garden.

Coleridge also sent the lines to Southey with the explanation that "I am a *Berkleian*" (*CL*, I, 335). Coleridge borrowed the second volume of Berkeley's *Works* from the Bristol Library in 1796, and in that volume *Siris* (1744) is the most considerable work.[9] *Siris* begins as a dissertation on the medicinal virtues of tar water and ascends the chain of being to a discussion of Platonic and Neoplatonic concepts of mind. In the final sections Berkeley gives a Platonic cast to his principle that existence is mental. Referring to Proclus, who divided philosophers into two camps, those who "placed Body first in the order of beings, and made the faculty of thinking depend thereupon," and those who made "corporeal things to be dependent upon Soul or Mind,"[10] Berkeley places himself in the latter group. The supreme mind is, of course, God, in whom all things have their perpetual creation. Sensations are fleeting phenomena, not to be known with certainty,[11] and thus the intellect must rise above mere sensation to perceive the permanent One. And insofar as the intellect is able to do this "we touch the divine Intellect." From the assumption that all existence is mental, Berkeley enumerates several doctrines that must have been congenial to Coleridge's hopes of finding himself a unified being: "According to the Platonic philosophy, *ens* and *unum* are the same. And consequently our minds participate so far of existence as they do of unity. But it should seem that personality is the indivisible centre of the soul or mind, which is a monad so far forth as she is

[9]For Coleridge's reading during the Somerset years, see George Whalley's "The Bristol Library Borrowings of Southey and Coleridge, 1793–8," *Library*, 4 (1949), 114–32. For the importance of *Siris* in Coleridge's reading, see Beer, p. 107.

[10]Berkeley, V, 124.

[11]Ibid., pp. 140–41.

a person. Therefore person is really that which exists, inasmuch as it participates of the divine unity."[12]

Philosophically, then, Coleridge found a context helpful in asserting that he was an active being, who, in rising above the knowledge of mere sensation without losing the sense of outness that it provided, could discover a ground for his being in God, and in so doing could create the unity and identity of his personality. With Berkeley's immaterialism he is assured that his perceptions of the exterior world repose also in the mind of God and is thus released from the fear of subjectivity, the fear of the "idle flitting phantasies" of "The Eolian Harp."

At the end of "This Lime-Tree Bower," Coleridge returns to the garden with an assurance he did not possess when he felt himself imprisoned there. In fact, he is seeing nature directly for the first time. Having established the priority of his imagination and the operation of imagination in other minds, he opens his eyes to see whether the physical reality of the garden will corroborate his imagination:

> Pale beneath the blaze
> Hung the transparent foliage; and I watch'd
> Some broad and sunny leaf, and lov'd to see
> The shadow of the leaf and stem above
> Dappling its sunshine! And that walnut-tree
> Was richly ting'd, and a deep radiance lay
> Full on the ancient ivy, which usurps
> Those fronting elms, and now, with blackest mass
> Makes their dark branches gleam a lighter hue
> Through the late twilight. . . .
>
> [ll. 47–56]

His mode of seeing the lime-tree bower is conditioned by the way he has imagined the landscape that Lamb and the Wordsworths have seen.[13] The "transparent foliage" is pale, like the "few poor yellow leaves" of the ash that hangs over the waterfall. Some of the leaves are dappled in the sunshine as are those that form the roof of the "roaring dell." At evening Lamb sees the entire landscape gilded by the setting sun; Coleridge sees the walnut tree colored by the same light, a light that makes the elms "gleam a lighter hue." Furthermore, the murmur of the bees relieves the silence in the garden, just as in the isolation of the dell animation is supplied by the movement

[12] Ibid., p. 156.

[13] For the scene in Poole's garden as an example of Coleridge's doctrine of the reconciliation of opposites, see Richard Harter Fogle's *The Idea of Coleridge's Criticism* (Berkeley and Los Angeles: Univ. of Calif. Press, 1962), pp. 28–33.

of the waterfall. All nature in the garden is now perceived to partake in the omnipresence of joy and life. The bower ceases to be a mere vacuum; he has verified his imagination.

Coleridge often begins with a sense of loss and attempts to overcome that loss of sensation and imprisonment in a particular spot by an act of his imagination that must be tested upon visible reality. In contrast, Wordsworth characteristically begins his poetic meditations with immediate sensation and then moves to a visionary insight. In "Tintern Abbey," to take a familiar example in the conversational mode, Wordsworth returns from an absence to survey the Wye Valley and then moves back in memory, building up associations until he transforms sensations into thoughts. To Wordsworth, place is often a source of vitality; to Coleridge it is a stasis that must be transcended by the active mind. And, significantly for Coleridge's conversational mode, he requires the mediation of other minds to reach the one mind of God.

Coleridge learns two lessons from his mental progress. The first is that "'Tis well to be bereft of promis'd good," because he is forced to contemplate the "joys we cannot share." What stimulates Coleridge's imagination in this poem is the initial frustration. The second lesson follows from the first:

> No plot so narrow, be but Nature there,
> No waste so vacant, but may well employ
> Each faculty of sense, and keep the heart
> Awake to Love and Beauty!
>
> [ll. 61–64]

What Coleridge affirmed in "This Lime-Tree Bower" he could not affirm in "Frost at Midnight." Like "This Lime-Tree Bower," "Frost at Midnight" begins with Coleridge in a vacuum, this time imprisoned by his separation from the motions of nature and the society of the cottage's other "inmates," a word that at the end of the eighteenth century referred to strangers dwelling in one's house. He discovers that he cannot overcome his isolation and becomes reconciled to the mysterious silence only by being able to hope that his son Hartley, whose upbringing will be quite different from his own, will be blessed with the insight to see plenitude and joy within apparent silence and inactivity.

"Frost at Midnight" is about the relationship of the early development of the child to the knowledge and insight of the adult. Its time scheme is similar to that of "Tintern Abbey," where Wordsworth returns to a spot he had visited in childhood to discover in the sensations from nature the sources of his present joy and liberation. But whenever Coleridge thinks of his own past, he thinks of his separation not only from nature but, more importantly, from human society; his recollections of his school days do not liberate him. Written at the time he was completing "The Ancient Mariner," "Frost at Midnight" reveals a discontinuity between his childhood hopes and the realities of adulthood.

At first Coleridge is confined by a vacancy and quiet that "disturbs / And vexes meditation." He hears the owlet's cry and his son's gentle breathing and sees the sooty film flutter on the grate, but he cannot apprehend the frost's ministry and the "numberless goings-on of life." In "This Lime-Tree Bower" the animation of the ash by the waterfall and the breaking of the evening silence by the murmur of the bees were sufficient evidence of the omnipresence of nature, but here the occasional sounds are cause for vexation. They emphasize the silence which they punctuate, a silence that is to him an unintelligible dream. The problem is not a failure of sensation, as it seems to be at the beginning of "This Lime-Tree Bower," for he is able to feel that animate things are companionable to him; he cannot comprehend the strange dreamlike vacuity. The puzzling calm frustrates his musings. Since he cannot know the dream through direct, verifiable sensation or through his normal process of thought, he is at a loss to understand it at all. His recollection of looking at the sooty film also does not help because the memories that came to him in childhood were likewise dreams.

The various texts of the poem from its first publication in 1798 until the final version indicate Coleridge's differing statements of his relationship to the film. In the first printed version Coleridge says that the flame is a

> companionable form,
> With which I can hold commune. Idle thought!
> But still the living spirit in our frame,
> That loves not to behold a lifeless thing,
> Transfuses into all its own delights,
> Its own volition, sometimes with deep faith
> And sometimes with fantastic playfulness.
>
> [*PW*, I, 240]

The only activity he recognizes is that of his own mind; even the film itself is a "lifeless thing" whose motion comes from the observer's eye. And he is wary of ascribing the movement in nature to nature's ministry. Sometimes he transfuses the delights "with deep faith," yet at other times it is only with "fantastic playfulness," that kind of playfulness which creates only phantasies. Coleridge is cautious about committing himself to a connection with the processes of nature and often fears that such a connection may be merely his own fanciful vision.

That this section gave Coleridge the most trouble is indicated by its being the most revised portion of the poem. He printed another version in *The Poetical Register* for 1808–09, not published until 1812, and tried again to formulate the relationship between the mind and the

> companionable form
> With which I can hold commune: haply hence,
> That still the living spirit in our frame,
> Which loves not to behold a lifeless thing,
> Transfuses into all things its own Will,
> And its own pleasures; sometimes with deep faith,
> And sometimes with a wilful playfulness
> That stealing pardon from our common sense
> Smiles, as self-scornful, to disarm the scorn
> For these wild reliques of our childish Thought,
> That flit about, oft go, and oft return
> Not uninvited.
>
> [*PW*, I, 241]

The dreams of the "living spirit" dissolve in the light of common sense. The only way he is able to deflect the intrusive intellect is to consider the creations of the mind "wild reliques of our childish Thought," which, like the phantasies in "The Eolian Harp," "flit about, oft go, and oft return."

Finally he shortened the section so that the

> idling Spirit
> By its own moods interprets, every where
> Echo or mirror seeking of itself,
> And makes a toy of thought.
>
> [ll. 20–23]

The only improvement is that the apologetic lines are removed. The difficulties inherent in regarding the motions of the "idling spirit" as "wild reliques of our childish Thought" are deleted, and the toys of thought are laughed off as amusing playthings.

The transition to the second verse paragraph in the version in *The Poetical Register* suggests that a loss has occurred. Having thought of the relics of childish thought, he naturally associates them with his superstitious gaze at the sooty film at school and the correspondent anticipation of the arrival of an absent friend:

> Ah there was a time,
> When oft amused by no such subtle toys

Of the self-watching mind, a child at school,
With most believing superstitious wish
Presageful, have I gazed on the bars. . . .

[*PW*, I, 241]

The use of the phrase "there was a time" recalls the context in which Coleridge[14] had used it in "The Mad Monk":

There was a time when earth, and sea, and skies,
  The bright green vale, and forest's dark recess,
With all things, lay before mine eyes
  In steady loveliness:
But now I feel, on earth's uneasy scene,
  Such sorrows as will never cease. . . .

[ll. 9–14]

And in the same context it appears in "Dejection":

There was a time when, though my path was rough,
  This joy within me dallied with distress,
And all misfortunes were but as the stuff
  Whence Fancy made me dreams of happiness. . . .

[ll. 76–79]

The similarity of the phrase to the opening lines of the "Immortality Ode" is obvious, and all of Coleridge's uses point to a sharp division between the experiences of the child and those of the adult. What separates the adult from the child is the "self-watching mind," the isolating self-consciousness of the adult. The child can believe in the dream, but the adult cannot indulge in superstition.

At school the film foretells of a reunion with absent friends. The recollection of the village scene feeds his hopes for companionship and promises the coming of distant friends. So long as his ability to dream facilitates his hope, he still expects to be visited. But no one arrives; his childhood expectations are frustrated. Coleridge reaches a dead end in his adult meditations, and his thoughts end in silence. Having been thrown back into the vacancy in which he began, he has not achieved a progressive understanding of the world around him, nor has he resolved his earlier vexation. The transition from the second to the third verse paragraph emphasizes his vacancy. He is awakened from the silence into which he had fallen by the breathing he hears in the "deep calm." But the word *deep* was added in the Errata of *Sibylline Leaves;* the earlier phrase, written while he was at work on "The Ancient Mariner," was the "dead calm." And in both

[14]For a discussion of the authorship, see Stephen M. Parrish and David V. Erdman, "Who Wrote *The Mad Monk?* A Debate," *BNYPL*, 64 (1960), 209–37.

the earlier and later versions Hartley's breathings "Fill up the interspersèd vacancies / And momentary pauses of the thought." The return to the present calm causes Coleridge to cast one final glance back to his childhood, a glance that further accounts for his present confinement: "I was reared / In the great city, pent 'mid cloisters dim, / And saw nought lovely but the sky and stars." The childhood that moments ago had appeared as replete with dreams is now a prison where he was barred from any significant contact with nature. The distance between the cloister walls and the infinitely remote stars implies the fate of his unfulfilled dreams.

Coleridge becomes reconciled to the silence and calm around him, not by assuring himself that he understands it, but by hoping that Hartley will. Hartley will "see and hear / The lovely shapes and sounds intelligible / Of that eternal language, which thy God / Utters." He will not be inhibited by the "self-watching mind" and will receive, not merely a promise of fulfillment, but fulfillment itself, because his education in nature will be different from his father's imprisonment away from it:

> Therefore all seasons shall be sweet to thee,
> Whether the summer clothe the general earth
> With greenness, or the redbreast sit and sing
> Betwixt the tufts of snow on the bare branch
> Of mossy apple-tree, while the nigh thatch
> Smokes in the sun-thaw; whether the eave-drops fall
> Heard only in the trances of the blast,
> Or if the secret ministry of frost
> Shall hang them up in silent icicles,
> Quietly shining to the quiet Moon.
>
> [ll. 65–74]

These lines are as lovely a natural description as Coleridge ever wrote. As earlier in the poem, there is no failure of sensation or of Coleridge's ability to organize imagery. But the way in which he organizes the imagery reveals that Hartley will be able to penetrate the mystery of the "secret ministry of frost," whereas to Coleridge it remains a mystery. Previously Coleridge had heard the momentary call of the owl and his son's breathing while the frost worked "unhelped by any wind" (l. 2), and Hartley will hear the sound of the falling eavedrops when there is a cessation of the blast. Up to this point Hartley's and his father's receptivity to nature are similar, but when there is no sound whatever in the chilled hush of evening, when the frost arrests the movement of the eavedrops and freezes them into icicles, Hartley will read the divine language which articulates the vision of the light from the moon and the reflected light of the icicles.

The quietude in the final lines is symbolic of fullness to Hartley, but to Coleridge the total significance behind the clearly apprehended sensation, the empirical evidence of the ministry, is still a secret.

In this final prayerful hope for his son's growth, Coleridge is able to forget his own disappointment, but only through thinking of someone else's joy can he reach any of his own. His expectations of being able to respond directly to nature are not satisfied in the final image of the frost. Coleridge resides outside the unity formed by Hartley and nature. There is still the gap between his puzzlement at the dreamlike presence of life and Hartley's intuitive understanding of it.

"The Nightingale," the only poem explicitly called a Conversation Poem, has the quietest tone of any of this group. Coleridge seems unwilling to engage in personal insights and is content to remain aloof as a guide to point out the beauties that others may experience. There is, too, a greater variety of tone in the veiled humor, which is directed against Coleridge himself. Resting with his friends upon a bridge over a silently flowing stream on an April night, he hears the nightingale's song, which reminds him of Milton's line "Most musical, most melancholy bird":

> A melancholy bird? Oh! idle thought!
> In Nature there is nothing melancholy.
> But some night-wandering man whose heart was pierced
> With the remembrance of a grievous wrong,
> Or slow distemper, or neglected love,
> (And so, poor wretch! filled all things with himself,
> And made all gentle sounds tell back the tale
> Of his own sorrow) he, and such as he,
> First named these notes a melancholy strain.
>
> [ll. 14–22]

Caught, a little embarrassed perhaps, between Wordsworth's belief in the virtues of immediate experience and horror of vicarious and bookish inspiration on the one hand, and the idol of Milton on the other, Coleridge felt he had to excuse his use of the line: "This passage in Milton possesses an excellence far superior to that of mere description; it is spoken in the character of the melancholy Man, and has therefore a *dramatic* propriety. The Author makes this remark, to rescue himself from the charge of having alluded with levity to a line in Milton" (*PW*, I, 264). But part of the humor of this passage rests on a knowledge of Coleridge's earlier poem, "To the Nightingale" (1795), in which he comes very close to falling into the traditional fiction of the melancholy song:

> How many wretched Bards address *thy* name,
> And hers, the full-orb'd Queen that shines above.

But I *do* hear thee, and the high bough mark,
Within whose mild moon-mellow'd foliage hid
Thou warblest sad thy pity-pleading strains.
O! I have listen'd, till my working soul,
Waked by those strains to thousand phantasies,
Absorb'd hath ceas'd to listen!

[ll. 7–14]

"The Nightingale" is organized in three roughly parallel scenes, each containing an individual in the presence of nature: Coleridge and his friends on the bridge at night, the "gentle Maid" in the grove, and finally Hartley in the presence of the moon. The first of these scenes is contrasted with the second two, which are strikingly alike in that both offer a picture of an individual participating in joyous communion with the moon.

The first, perhaps not surprisingly, opens with a setting described wholly in negatives:

No cloud, no relique of the sunken day
Distinguishes the West, no long thin slip
Of sullen light, no obscure trembling hues.

[ll. 1–3]

The stream beneath the bridge is seen in a "glimmer" but is not heard, and the stars above are dimmed by the clouds that offer showers in compensation for their obscuring the stars. The moon, which in the other two scenes emerges from behind the clouds to bring a sudden moment of inspiration, is not mentioned, being hidden by the clouds. Coleridge hears the bird's song and thinks of youths who spend their spring evenings in "ball-rooms and hot theatres" and the melancholy poet who should stretch

his limbs
Beside a brook in mossy forest-dell,
By sun or moon-light, to the influxes
Of shapes and sounds and shifting elements
Surrendering his whole spirit, of his song
And of his fame forgetful!

[ll. 25–30]

The youth, who surrenders his whole spirit, like Coleridge in "The Eolian Harp," who stretches his limbs on the hillside, is a type of the harp, a figure that recurs often in these poems. The harp image here, however, is not personalized as it is earlier. Coleridge has learned to abstract himself from it and does so with the commonplace that he and the Wordsworths "may not thus profane / Nature's sweet voices." The bird's song, which is emphasized by the silence, recalls other similar scenes in which the symbol of the harp is implicit, but none of them involve him as a part of the symbol. In a move characteristic of the other poems, he shifts from an actual scene in which the moon is not present to an imagined one where the moon sails out from behind the clouds. He tries to apply the lesson he learned in "This Lime-Tree Bower," that "'Tis well to be bereft of promis'd good," but unlike that poem there is no return to the present.

The song of the nightingale heard in the April evening reminds Coleridge of another spot, "a castle huge, / Which the great lord inhabits not," where the formal gardens have reverted to the wilderness of natural growth so that the birds have made it their home. A "most gentle Maid" who lives near the spot is the spirit of the place, the goddess of the grove. An intimate of the birds, she knows all of their songs. Hers has been the joy of hearing, after a moment's silence, the sudden burst of song when the moon shines on the garden. The moon

> Emerging, hath awakened earth and sky
> With one sensation, and those wakeful birds
> Have all burst forth in choral minstrelsy,
> As if some sudden gale had swept at once
> A hundred airy harps! And she hath watched
> Many a nightingale perch giddily
> On blossomy twig still swinging from the breeze,
> And to that motion tune his wanton song
> Like tipsy Joy that reels with tossing head.
>
> [ll. 78–86]

The birds surrender themselves to the light in a joyous dance. In the *Philosophical Lectures,* Coleridge said that in joy, individuality, the consciousness of oneself as being separate from nature, "is lost and it therefore is liveliest in youth" (*PL,* p. 179). Each nightingale possesses no consciousness of itself as a being separate from the joyous chorus of the other birds and the animating influence of the moonlight.

The final repetition of the harp symbol is Coleridge's holding his son up to the moon:

> once, when he awoke
> In most distressful mood (some inward pain
> Had made up that strange thing, an infant's dream—)
> I hurried with him to our orchard-plot,
> And he beheld the moon, and, hushed at once,
> Suspends his sobs, and laughs most silently,
> While his fair eyes, that swam with undropped tears,
> Did glitter in the yellow moon-beam!
>
> [ll. 98–105]

The origin of this "father's tale" is found in Coleridge's notebook for 1797–98: "Hartley fell down & hurt himself—I caught him up crying & screaming—& ran out of doors with him.—The Moon caught his eye—he ceased crying immediately—& his eyes & the tears in them, how they glittered in the Moonlight" (*NB*, I, 219). The change in the cause of the tears, from a fall to the "infant's dream," is significant in the light of Coleridge's ambiguous attitude towards the dream. For Hartley the power of the moon quiets the disturbing dream. He received the healing and restorative moonlight presented to him as suddenly as it comes to the birds and the lady in the grove. In fact all three receive blessing while Coleridge himself is only a witness to it.

As in the other Conversation Poems written within a year of "The Nightingale," there are other centers of perception, other imaginations who sing a more exalted song in contrast to Coleridge's conversational tone. Seeing and recollecting having seen others associate joy with the night is not the same as experiencing it oneself, no matter how fully one sympathizes with others. Admittedly there is no explicit conflict between the minds and experiences that create the dialogue of the poem, but, nevertheless, Coleridge preserves the distinction between his and others' minds.

Coleridge begins these Conversation Poems in a calm, but it is not the calm of plenitude, a quiet repose when the heart listens. The calm is more often a threatening stasis, something to be overcome by an act of faith and the imagination. M. H. Abrams has called attention to the "emotional issue pressing for resolution" in many of the later romantic lyrics: Coleridge's "Dejection," Wordsworth's "Immortality Ode," Shelley's "Stanzas Written in Dejection," and "West Wind." The emotional problem, he says, is one of dejection, "a profound sadness, sometimes bordering on the anguish of terror or despair, at the sense of loss, dereliction, isolation, or inner death, which is presented as inherent in the conditions of the speaker's existence."[15] These early Conversation Poems do not begin in the deep despair with which "Dejection" opens—where Coleridge's only wish is for the storm to come and bring him pain to prove that there is still some life remaining in him. They do anticipate, however, some aspects of the later poems that Abrams mentions. The deprivation in "This Lime-Tree Bower" causes him to think of Lamb and the Wordsworths and thus to include their minds as an essential part in that imaginative response to nature. In yet other poems, "Frost at Midnight" being the best example, Coleridge's frustration at being separated from nature is not eased. He begins the movement toward

[15] Abrams, "Structure and Style in the Greater Romantic Lyric," pp. 552–53.

other minds only after he has examined his own past and has exhausted his own resources, whereas in "This Lime-Tree Bower" the exploration of his memory is undertaken simultaneously with the movement toward other minds.

Coleridge cannot sustain an unqualified assertion of his own comprehension of the mysteries of life. Only the mediation of other minds permits him to rise to unqualified assertion, and often at significant points his progress is arrested so that instead of realizing his participation in joy he learns of his own distance from it. The reconciliation with nature in "Frost at Midnight" is purchased at the price of a self-effacement which is a quiet resignation momentarily interrupted by his hopes for Hartley. Whether or not Coleridge himself succeeds in rising to unqualified assertion, he usually delivers a blessing on those who do, but even still the paradigm is not always followed and the symmetry of the poems is often left incomplete.

By April 1798, the date of "The Nightingale," he had completed his most optimistic poems in the conversational mode. "Dejection" and "To William Wordsworth" follow in a few years during which he had ceased to make optimistic statements about his own ability to construct a self, to find in his past and present the necessary continuity, and to ground that self in a greater personal reality whose existence he never doubted. He recognizes, in these poems, the fact that he is removed from that reality and seeks in the fact of separation an explanation for it. The answers were not always clear; many of them are found buried in his notebooks and are obscured by his own uncertainties about metaphysics. The conclusions that did come to him brought him close to an understanding of himself and to a theory of evil, much of the primary evidence for which is contained in "Kubla Khan" and "The Ancient Mariner," written in the same year as these Conversation Poems.

Chapter III

"Kubla Khan": That Phantom-World So Fair

COLERIDGE'S FAME as a poet rests on the achievement of the mystery poems, "Kubla Khan," "The Ancient Mariner," and "Christabel." The Conversation Poems, if they are known to a general audience, are regarded uncritically as minor efforts in a mode more properly Wordsworthian, even though they precede "Tintern Abbey" and clearly stand as a paradigm that Wordsworth varies. At first sight the easy conversational middle style and the presence of other persons seem quite different from the more pronounced artfulness and solitary vision of "Kubla Khan."

Although it appears to be the creation of an entirely different poet, "Kubla Khan" repeats several motifs of the Conversation Poems. It explores the relationship between the strength of the human imagination and the impulses with which it must work. In "This Lime-Tree Bower" the mind's creations liberate Coleridge from the state of mind in which he is incapable of responding to the immediate experience of nature and permit him to return to Poole's garden to verify his imagination. Imagination and nature in the garden are substantially the same. The images of the mind and the sensations from without are literally interchangeable. "Kubla Khan" further tests the imagination's validity. The order of the imagination depicted in the opening lines is united with the vitality of the garden, but, as in other, less optimistic Conversation Poems, the imaginative order is lost. At best there is a balance between the Khan's creation of the dome with its surrounding walls and the fertility of the river. Containment and control of the inspirational force are not sustained, because the dome vibrates on the surface of the river; the delightful dream is lost because order cannot be maintained. The final lines, though not a recantation as in the earlier Conversation Poems, still distance Coleridge from the vision, a distancing that anticipates the later distancing in "Frost at Midnight" and "The Nightingale."[1] Coleridge is

[1] I accept the date of October 1797 for "Kubla Khan" suggested by Griggs (*CL*, I, 348–49) and by E. K. Chambers, *Samuel Taylor Coleridge* (Oxford: Clarendon Press, 1938), pp. 100–103. In the Preface to the published poem (1816) Coleridge said that it was written in the summer of 1797, but in a note on the Crewe manuscript he says, "This fragment with a good deal more, not recoverable, composed, in a sort

removed from the intensity of the vision in "Kubla Khan," just as he was suspicious of his speculations in the earlier poems, and for the same reasons.

An explanation of how the delightful dream was lost is presented in the Preface. Whether "Kubla Khan" was in fact composed during an opium dream has been questioned, and the man from Porlock has long ago been dismissed as a Coleridgean attempt to belittle his own accomplishment and to make excuses for not satisfying his readers' expectations. But the Preface need not be accepted or rejected on the grounds of its literal truth; it can be taken seriously as Coleridge's attempt to explain one process of poetic creation and the inadequacies of that process which led to an inevitable loss. Both the Preface and the poem have creativity as their subjects; both trace, not only the creative process, but also the loss of creativity. Creation in this instance began when Coleridge had before him the objective reality of the sentence from Purchas: "Here the Khan Kubla commanded a palace to be built, and a stately garden thereunto. And thus ten miles of fertile ground were inclosed with a wall."[2] When Coleridge fell asleep, Purchas's words were transformed into visual imagery. The sleep itself was profound, "at least of the external senses," one in which the immediate surroundings were obscured but one in which the mind was still active. Images came to him "as *things*, with a parallel production of the correspondent expressions, without any sensation or consciousness of effort." The images appeared to be substantial realities, for he had no frame of reference that would prove them otherwise. Additionally, the sequence in which the images arose was an involuntary one.

That "Kubla Khan" was composed in a reverie is doubtful. To see the conscious art in the poem, we do not need Wordsworth's reminder that Coleridge was "quite an epicure in sound" and "that when he was intent on a new experiment in metre, the time and labour he bestowed were inconceivable."[3] Whether or not there ever

---

of Reverie brought on by two grains of Opium, taken to check a dysentery, at a Farm House between Porlock and Linton, a quarter of a mile from Culbone Church, in the fall of the year, 1797." See Shelton, pp. 32–42. For a criticism of the 1797 date, see Schneider, pp. 153–237, and support for her argument offered by Jean Robertson, "The Date of 'Kubla Khan,'" *RES*, 18 (1967), 438–39.

[2] *PW*, I, 296. The actual sentence, which E. H. Coleridge prints as a footnote, reads: "In Xamdu did Cublai Can build a stately Palace, encompassing sixteene miles of plaine ground with a wall, wherein are fertile Meddowes, pleasant Springs, delightfull Streames, and all sorts of beasts of chase and game, and in the middest thereof a sumptuous house of pleasure."

[3] Grosart, III, 427. The discovery of textual variants in "Kubla Khan" indicates Coleridge's care with its composition.

was a man from Porlock, the vision that was held so firmly in the dream was lost soon after awakening. The rest of the vision "passed away like the images on the surface of a stream into which a stone has been cast." The images that were apprehended vividly as things became insubstantial shadows that faded into nothingness, because, as Coleridge shows in the poem, the images were projected upon a medium which momentarily constituted their reality but which also proved they were nothing. To illustrate this loss, Coleridge added lines from "The Picture" to the Preface:

> Then all the charm
> Is broken—all that phantom-world so fair
> Vanishes, and a thousand circlets spread,
> And each mis-shape['s] the other. Stay awhile,
> Poor youth! who scarcely dar'st lift up thine eyes—
> The stream will soon renew its smoothness, soon
> The visions will return! And lo, he stays,
> And soon the fragments dim of lovely forms
> Come trembling back, unite, and now once more
> The pool becomes a mirror.
>
> [*PW*, I, 296]

But unlike the image of the lover in "The Picture," there was no "after restoration" of the images from his dream. That Coleridge, in his later years, and after his own sense of loss of poetic powers, could affix these lines to the Preface and dismiss the poem as a "psychological curiosity" indicate that he came to view it suspiciously. Just as the images of the dream were lost by interruption and because of their inherent unreality, the vision contained in the lines immediately written down was lost. The man from Porlock was a frequent visitor.

The poem opens abruptly with a picture of the dome. Coleridge dispenses with the frame that traditionally opens the conventional dream vision, such as the description of the poet's walking out on a May morning and falling asleep. The abruptness of the opening is effective, for the picture of the dome is not filtered through the hazy eyes of a dreamer. It is seen directly, and it is real. The Khan creates his paradise by decree, by willing it into being, a type of divine creation. Coleridge does not mention the building of the walls, towers, and dome as though they were built by a laborious human effort. The pleasure dome comes into being because the Khan has uttered the decree, the words of creation, and as the words are spoken the grounds are circumscribed. The pleasure of the gardens is not in the sensual indulgences permitted there, which are simply not mentioned in the poem, but in the joy, the deep delight of creation itself. The words of creation are immediately transformed into things, real objects, just as

Purchas's words rose before Coleridge as things, but, of course, the Khan's creation is willed.[4] The garden itself is an enclosed space in which it at first appears that all nature is tempered and controlled by human art. The Khan is an artist who has imposed solid architectural order upon the spontaneous garden. The whole enclosed space is a projection of the Khan's artistic imagination and an assertion of his essential individuality. The dome constitutes the center of the fruitfully limited field of consciousness; in this spot restriction and exclusion constitute a definition of the self and are in contrast to the deadness of imprisonment at the beginning of some of the Conversation Poems.[5]

But to the poet who apprehends the delightful dream, the image of the pleasure dome is a precarious one; its apparent permanence is as chimerical as the reflection of the image on the stream. The original order of the gardens is created by the balancing of antithetical forces: the artificial construction of the pleasure dome with its walls and the naturally disruptive forces of the river.[6] The initial vision of the pleasure grounds, which at first comprises both the order of the dome and the generative water, is held in the imagination. The pleasure dome at the center, with the source of the river on the one side and the "caverns measureless to man" on the other, is the central work that dominates and unifies the gardens. Its delight is its fertility, its blossoming and incense-bearing trees and sunny spots of greenery that are nurtured by the sacred river.

The river is sacred because it is the true source of generation and life. In Coleridge's notebook, four entries after the often-cited source in Maurice's *History of Hindostan* for the "caves of ice" passage are several that concern water symbolism. As Lowes suggests, Coleridge may at this time have been looking for material for his projected hymns to the sun, moon, and the four elements.[7] The first cryptic note reads "Water—Thales.—" (*NB*, I, 244). Coleridge may have been informed about Thales by Aristotle, who, in the *Metaphysics*, wrote that Thales believed the first cause is "water (for which reason he declared that the earth rests on water), getting the notion perhaps

[4]J. B. Beer reminds us "of the tradition that Kubla Khan constructed his palace according to a dream" (p. 331 n. 3). But Coleridge is either unaware of the tradition or deliberately changes it, for the Khan's creation is conscious.

[5]S. K. Heninger, Jr., offers a fascinating interpretation of the creation as a Jungian mandala in "A Jungian Reading of 'Kubla Khan,'" *JAAC*, 18 (1960), 358–67.

[6]R. H. Fogle sees "the core of the poem to reside in an opposition or stress between the garden, artificial and finite, and the indefinite, inchoate, and possibly turbulent outside world" ("The Romantic Unity of 'Kubla Khan,'" *CE*, 13 [1951], 15).

[7]Lowes, p. 379.

from seeing that the nutriment of all things is moist, and that heat itself is generated from the moist and kept alive by it."[8]

Coburn suggests some possible sources for entry 244 but does not mention Aristotle himself. The entries that follow in the notebook quote from the *Metaphysics* passages that are located quite near Aristotle's explanation of Thales' belief in the first cause, but Coburn points out that they are taken from Cudworth's *True Intellectual System.* What makes it tempting to speculate that Coleridge read the passage from Aristotle is Aristotle's statement that Thales believed that the earth rests on water. This idea corresponds with a similar one Lowes found in his reading of travel literature Coleridge used as a mine for his imagery. For instance, in Bruce's *Travels to Discover the Source of the Nile* (1790) Coleridge read of the fountains along the Nile:

> The second fountain lies about a stone-cast west from the first: the inhabitants say that *this whole mountain is full of water,* and add, that the whole plain about the fountain is floating and unsteady, a certain mark that there is water concealed under it; for which reason, the water does not overflow at the fountain, but *forces itself with great violence out* at the foot of the mountain. The inhabitants . . . maintain that that year it trembled little on account of the drought, but other years, that *it trembled and overflowed so as that it could scarce be approached without danger.*[9]

And in Bernier's *Voyage to Surat* Coleridge read:

> I left my way again, to approach a great lake, which I saw afar off, through the middle whereof passeth the river that runs to Baramoulay. . . . In the midst of this lake there is an eremitage with its little garden, which, as they say, *doth miraculously float upon the water.*[10]

Perhaps Coleridge associated these statements of the land's being supported by and floating on water with the quotation from the *Metaphysics.* All of them may be reflected in the cryptic notation about Thales. The images certainly were in his reading, but the significance he gives them is his own.

Whether or not Coleridge made such associations, the notebook entries which follow that on Thales continue the theme of generation. Two entries later Coleridge copied from Cudworth a passage from the *Metaphysics* which follows that in which Aristotle explains the belief in the primacy of water. Some believed

[8] *Metaphysics,* I, 3, in, *The Basic Works of Aristotle,* ed. Richard McKeon (New York: Random House, 1941), p. 694.

[9] Lowes, p. 372 (Lowes's italics).

[10] Ibid., p. 386 (Lowes's italics).

the Ocean and Tethys to have been the original of generation: and for this cause the oath of the gods is said to be by water (called by the poets Styx) as being that from which they all derived their original. For an oath ought to be by that which is most honourable; and that which is most ancient is most honourable.

[*NB*, I, 246n]

The allusion to those who thought that Ocean and Tethys were "the original of generation" is specifically to Homer's line "The father of all gods the ocean is, Tethys their mother," which in the original Greek constitutes entry 247. The hymns were never written, but the annotations indicate that if they were, water would have been praised as the force of generation, the most ancient and venerable of the gods. Perhaps, also, Coleridge did not write the poems because he had already used the material in "Kubla Khan" and "The Ancient Mariner."

The fountain from which the river flows is described in terms of human sexuality and generation:

> But oh! that deep romantic chasm which slanted
> Down the green hill athwart a cedarn cover!
> A savage place! as holy and enchanted
> As e'er beneath a waning moon was haunted
> By woman wailing for her demon-lover!
> And from this chasm, with ceaseless turmoil seething,
> As if this earth in fast thick pants were breathing,
> A mighty fountain momently was forced:
> Amid whose swift half-intermitted burst
> Huge fragments vaulted like rebounding hail,
> Or chaffy grain beneath the thresher's flail:
> And 'mid these dancing rocks at once and ever
> It flung up momently the sacred river.

[ll. 12–24]

Unlike the Khan's creation by decree, instantaneous and so out of time, this creation is continuous in time, one that is accompanied by the pains and tumult of human birth. The fecundity of earth is echoed later in Coleridge's adaptation of Stolberg's *Hymne an die Erde:* "Earth! thou mother of numberless children, the nurse and the mother. . ." The metric regularity of the first eleven lines of "Kubla Khan" is broken into the irregularity of lines twelve to twenty to convey the physical sensation of labored effort. Many of the lines have feminine rhyme, and at significant points spondees are substituted for iambs: "with ceaseless turmoil seething" and "in fast thick pants were breathing." A prefatory note to "Hymn to the Earth" discusses the difficulty of writing hexameters in English because of the paucity of true spondees. As an example of one of the few in English, Coleridge cites *turmoil*, a further echo of "Kubla Khan."

The river also has a further significance. It represents the sources of the unconscious. Both its origin and destination are unknowable and are common symbols for the unconscious. The explosive force with which the river erupts into the serenity of the garden from an unknown source and, after flowing at random, returns "through caverns measureless to man / Down to a sunless sea" indicates that while it provides the essential fertility, it also threatens tranquillity and order. Within the garden it meanders at its own will until it cascades "in tumult to a lifeless ocean." These random movements are quite similar to those implied in Coleridge's consistent references to the random flow of images through his mind. The illustration of the imagination by the figure of the water insect that is both active and passive (*BL*, I, 85–86) pertains to the relationship of the active mind to the flow of images. The water provides the materials upon which the imagination must work, materials which, while they are necessary to fertility and generation, are also potentially dangerous if they are not properly controlled. Coleridge is beginning to realize the inimical influence of an irresistible force working upon him, and he is beginning to understand that that irresistible force which he had formerly called the One Life may originate in unfathomable depths of his own mind.

Having described the origin and ultimate destination of the river, Coleridge returns to the dome itself, which has assumed a different appearance:

> The shadow of the dome of pleasure
> Floated midway on the waves;
> Where was heard the mingled measure
> From the fountain and the caves.
> It was a miracle of rare device,
> A sunny pleasure-dome with caves of ice.
>
> [ll. 31–36]

In the first printed edition of the poem in 1816, these lines are separated from the previous verse paragraph.[11] The shortened lines and the reestablished metrical regularity recall the regularity of the first seven lines, in which the stable creation is first presented. But the stability is not completely restored. It is difficult to know exactly how to visualize the image of the dome. It may be that we are to see the dome itself in the midst of the river upon a floating island as described by Bernier. But it is the "shadow" of the dome that floats on

[11]The lines are not separated in the Crewe MS. See Shelton.

the waves, apparently not the dome itself. The word *shadow* may here refer to an image or reflection of the dome, for the whole scene is a "sunny pleasure-dome with caves of ice."[12] In the light of the prefatory quotation from "The Picture," the second reading is the better one. The caves of ice themselves may be either under the dome itself or in the river. Earlier in the poem the caverns are located at the point at which the river drops into the "sunless sea." However one visualizes the image, the balance between the dome and the river is so precarious that it is difficult to speak of it as a reconciliation of opposites. The miracle is that there is such a delicate balance, one that is threatened at every moment. Because of the turbulence of the river, there is no permanent solidity. The "mingled measure" that is heard comes from the "ceaseless turmoil" of the fountain, where the woman wails for her demon lover, and from the river's falling into the sunless sea from which Kubla heard voices "prophesying war."

Order and harmony are threatened by the power of the river. The dome is apprehended as a mere vibrating shadow, not a "thing," as Coleridge used the word in the Preface; previously it had been a solid reality. As an image its existence is rendered unstable by the very material upon which it is projected, the water which sustains it momentarily but which eventually dissolves it. If the lines from "The Picture" are an accurate description of the loss of vision, then the existence of the image on the water, and indeed the entire poem, is merely momentary. The vision fails, then, not primarily because the poet is limited in his powers to perceive a transcendental reality, but because the materials that compose the vision are inherently unstable.

If we are to take seriously Coleridge's declaration that the poem as we have it was conceived in his dream and transcribed immediately after awakening, then the final eighteen lines originally comprised a part of that vision. In such a view the poem is the fragmentary beginning of a much longer poem that was lost at the point Coleridge was invoking the Abyssinian maid as he would a muse. But a more sensible view is that the last lines are a commentary upon his inability to continue the first thirty-six line vision of the dome and to regard the Preface as misleading on this point. The first two lines in the final verse paragraph refer to a vision prior to the opium dream: "A damsel with a dulcimer / In a vision once I saw . . ." The subtitle, "A Vision in a Dream," refers most directly to the vision of

[12] I agree with Shelton's reading of the word *shadow* and his criticism (pp. 35–36) of Beer's contention that "the dome of pleasure is not the pleasure-dome which Kubla decreed" (p. 246).

the dome itself, and although there are symbolic similarities between the two, they are distinct.

Coleridge says that he "would build that dome in air, / That sunny dome! Those caves of ice!" if only he could revive within himself the song of the Abyssinian maid. If he could revive the song, he could restore the certainty of vision that he initially imaged the Khan possessing, a certainty that the images of the dream constituted a reality. Thus equipped, he could continue to write prophetic poetry and would become the inspired poet of the final lines. But the voice in the last eighteen lines is subjunctive, and the statement hypothetical; he cannot revive the song. The poetic visions after "Kubla Khan," "The Ancient Mariner" and "Christabel," possess their solidity in the central images, but ironically the dreams reveal symbols of evil, not of deep delight.

To renew the dream would indeed be a deep delight for Coleridge —yet it is not renewed, nor does the hypothetical tone of the last lines indicate that Coleridge will try to recover it. Structurally, this presentation of the lost dream resembles some of the Conversation Poems. The endings of both the Conversation Poems and "Kubla Khan" qualify the aspirations expressed in the earlier sections and suggest the problems of fulfilling the promise of vision. Certainly "Kubla Khan" does not explicitly disavow the airy speculations as "The Eolian Harp" does, nor is there a veiled withdrawal so that others may realize the expectations as in "Frost at Midnight." Coleridge's inability to retain the vision does not come from any fear that the pleasure dome is morally inadequate as was retirement in "Reflections on Having Left a Place of Retirement." Even though Purchas describes the pleasure gardens as the construction of an Oriental despot who selfishly builds a palace of sensual pleasure, the poem itself does not emphasize those qualities. The dome is stately, and the word *pleasure,* which is constantly used in conjunction with the dome, refers to the delight of poetic creativity.

Coleridge cannot recapture the dome because he lacks the "symphony and song" of the Abyssinian maid, the necessary prerequisite for attaining the vision. When he laments the loss of his imagination in "Dejection," he explains that the loss of joy had dried up the sources of vitality and likens joy to "this strong music in the soul" (l. 60). Yet music was for him not always emblematic of spontaneous, natural joy. "Music is the most entirely human of the fine arts," he wrote in "On Poesy or Art," "and has the fewest *analoga* in nature" (*BL,* II, 261). He must regain the conscious and deliberately artful control to counteract the inspirational turmoil that comes from the fountain and the caves and must further harmonize the "mingled measure" the Khan hears. The presence of the Abyssinian maid invites comparison of her with the "woman wailing for her demon-lover." If the maid's song represents the imaginative order that is a precondition of art and vision, then she is contrasted with the woman wailing in uncontrolled passion and desire. Even so the exotic qualities of the maid also type her as a symbol of inspiration, a characteristic that is emphasized, not in Coleridge's picture of her, but in the portrait of someone inspired by her:

And all who heard should see them there,
And all should cry, Beware! Beware!
His flashing eyes, his floating hair!
Weave a circle round him thrice,
And close your eyes with holy dread,
For he on honey-dew hath fed,
And drunk the milk of Paradise.

[ll. 48–54]

The figure of the frenzied poet is at least as old as Plato's *Ion,* in which Ion delivers his lines without conscious understanding of their meaning. To become such a poet would necessitate a surrender to the powerful flow of inspiration represented by the river. Thus although the maid seems to embody the same balance of artful control and vital inspiration as in the dome and gardens in the first stanza, Coleridge is wary of her because he fears the effect of inspiration upon him. In "Reflections on Having Left a Place of Retirement," Coleridge rejected a false paradise in hopes of gaining a truer one; here he stands back from the Abyssinian paradise that is the gateway to another, more delightful vision.

Looking through that gateway and thinking what his creation would be like were he to enter, Coleridge believes that his would be a "dome in air" which would depend upon his song for its continued existence. He wrote to Poole from Germany that he "could half suspect that what are deemed fine descriptions, produce their effects almost purely by a charm of words, with which & with whose combinations, we associate *feelings* indeed, but no distinct *Images*" (*CL,* I, 511). There is the temptation to read this comment, and others like it, as a gloss upon the dome in air and to believe that the dimness of the image and its ethereality are positive achievements for Coleridge.[13] But the symbolic framework of the poem indicates that for an image to be indistinct or unstable is for it to be lost in the strong

[13]Schneider, pp. 277–78. She argues against a symbolic reading but for a reading in which the beauty of the poem is its music and its vague but suggestive imagery. While I avoid symbolic readings as she does, I do not wish to rest Coleridge's claim to

current of feelings. The voyage back to the original solidity of the Khan's dome is long and dangerous, and Coleridge knows that the closest he can come is "that dome in air." The reference of "that dome" is to the reflection of the original given in the first eleven lines, the vivid definition of Kubla's individuality, a definition that sets the proper bounds to his self without a proud self-assertion which defies divinity.

Could he approach the original image, it would win him the "deep delight." While he seems reluctant to surrender himself to the inspiration presented by the Abyssinian maid, he can still entertain thoughts of the deep joy that would accompany his assuming the prophetic role. The role is assumed, and the images that the mind creates are vivid realities in "The Ancient Mariner." But the deep delight he anticipates turns to fear and dread as his capturing, or rather his being captured by, the dream images that the mariner presents to the wedding guest constitutes a "dear ransom" of his individuality. He obtains not the individuality of a fruitful balance between the conscious and the unconscious, but a total extinction of personality.

---

greatness solely upon the incantatory beauty of the poem. And although I speak here and elsewhere in terms of images, the images are symbolic in the Coleridgean sense that they constitute the reality that they represent, but that reality is not a spiritual one in the poetry. It is a mental reality, reflecting what is actually in the poet's, or speaker's, mind.

Chapter IV

The Mariner's Nightmare

THE COMMENTS OF Coleridge's contemporaries about the genesis of "The Ancient Mariner" reveal that his initial interest was in depicting the nightmare state, not, as so many modern critics have maintained, in a desire to describe a spiritual voyage to transcendental knowledge or a heightened awareness of the spiritual force of the universe. Wordsworth told the Reverend Alexander Dyce that the poem "was founded on a strange dream which one of Coleridge's friends had, who fancied he saw a skeleton ship, with figures in it."[1] The poem most likely arose, as De Quincey was informed by Wordsworth, whom he called a man of "stern veracity," in Coleridge's plan to write "a poem on delirium, confounding its own dream-scenery with external things, and connected with the imagery of high latitudes."[2] If De Quincey and Wordsworth are correct, Coleridge's purpose was to follow the emotions of a man who in a delirium believed himself under a curse and persecuted by supernatural forces;[3] the interest was not in the supernatural itself but in the mental aberrations of a person who thought that the supernatural was a reality independent of his own mind. "The excellence aimed at," Coleridge explained in Chapter XIV of the *Biographia*, "was to consist in the interesting of the affections by the dramatic truth of such emotions, as would naturally accompany such situations, supposing them real. And real in *this* sense they have been to every human being who, from whatever source of delusion, has at any time believed himself under supernatural agency" (*BL,* II, 5).

At the end of Chapter XIII, which contains the enigmatic definition of imagination, Coleridge promised an essay on "the uses of the Supernatural in poetry" (*BL,* I, 202). A shadow seems to have fallen between the conception and the birth of this essay, but perhaps Cole-

[1] *The Reminiscences of Alexander Dyce,* ed. Richard J. Schrader (Columbus: Ohio State Univ. Press, 1972), p. 185.

[2] *Collected Writings of Thomas De Quincey,* ed. D. Masson (London: Black, 1889–90), II, 145.

[3] See Grosart, III, 442: Wordsworth said, "We agreed to write jointly a poem, the subject of which Coleridge took from a dream which a friend of his had once dreamt concerning a person suffering under a dire curse from the commission of some crime."

ridge did not bother to collect the various notes he made for it because its major point was offered in the opening paragraphs of the next chapter. Were the essay compiled from his notes, it would probably not differ essentially from the points he makes at the beginning of Chapter XIV. Coburn prints in *Inquiring Spirit* a note that must have been intended for that essay:

In poetry, whether metrical or unbound, the super-natural will be impressive and obtain a mastery over the Imagination and feelings, will tend to infect the reader, and draw him to identify himself with, or substitute himself for, the *Person* of the Drama or Tale, in proportion as it is true *to Nature*—i.e. when the Poet of his free will and judgement does what the Believing Narrator of a Supernatural Incident, Apparition or Charm does from ignorance and weakness of mind,—i.e. mistake a *Subjective* product (A saw the Ghost of Z) for an objective fact—the Ghost of Z was there to be seen; or by the magnifying and modifying power of Fear and *dreamy* Sensations, and the additive and supplementary interpolations of the *creative* Memory and the inferences and comments of the prejudiced Judgement slipt consciously into and confounded with the *Text* of the actual experience, exaggerates an unusual Natural event or appearance into the Miraculous and supernatural.

The Poet must always be in perfect sympathy with the Subject of the Narrative, and tell his tale with "a most believing mind"; but the Tale will be then most impressive for all when it is so constructed and particularized with such [traits?] and circumstances, that the Psychologist and thinking Naturalist shall be furnished with the Means of explaining it as a possible fact, by distinguishing and assigning the *Subjective* portion to its true power.[4]

Even Wordsworth, whose critical note to the 1800 text was severe, admitted that the poem "contains many delicate touches of passion, and indeed the passion is every where true to nature" (*LB*, p. 277).

Coleridge used the materials from his own experience to compose the mariner's reverie. The poem is a willed, organized, and artful portrait of a man who labors under the illusion that he is suffering under a curse. Coleridge's interest in the psychology of the mariner's dream continued after the poem's publication in 1798. Perhaps further informed by his own observations on dreams and nightmares and spurred on by the critics' complaints of obscurity, Coleridge revised throughout the poem, but the most extensive revisions occurred in the third section, the appearance of the specter ship. In 1798 the skeleton was little more than a gothic horror:

His bones were black with many a crack,
All black and bare, I ween;

[4]Notebook 43, printed in *Inquiring Spirit,* ed. Kathleen Coburn (London: Routledge, 1951), p. 191. The entry is dated May 1830. The phrase "a most believing mind" is from "Frost at Midnight" (l. 24).

Jet-black and bare, save where with rust
Of mouldy damps and charnel crust
They're patch'd with purple and green.

. . . . .

A gust of wind sterte up behind
And whistled thro' his bones;
Thro' the holes of his eyes and the hole of his mouth
Half-whistles and half-groans.

[ll. 181–85, 195–98]

He does not convey the terror that Coleridge felt was necessary to the strange dream; it is merely thrilling, an example of what Wordsworth in the Preface to *Lyrical Ballads* called "gross and violent stimulants," and leads one to think that the mariner had been reading too many "frantic novels" (*WPW*, II, 389).

One cannot be sure exactly when the major revisions for the 1817 text were made, but some reasonably accurate guesses can be made from the information contained in Coburn's edition of the *Notebooks*. She mentions that as Coleridge's own feelings of depression and isolation deepened toward the end of 1803 and on the voyage to Malta in 1804, he came to associate himself with his creation, the mariner becalmed on a dead sea (*NB*, II, 1996n). It is always dangerous to equate the creator with his creation, and particularly so with the identification of Coleridge with his mariner. The mariner seems not to comprehend what happens to him, and the spectral and angelic visions confuse him. Coleridge the poet did understand what happened to the mariner, and after 1800, as his knowledge of the nightmare increased, he was better able to render an accurate picture of that state.

Observations he made on the voyage to Malta, conditioned as they were by his recollection of his own poem, gave him phrases and images that he later added. In May 1804 he used the phrase "the Star, that dogged the Crescent" (*NB*, II, 2060) to describe an object of the sailors' superstition, a phrase that was later to be slightly altered to "the star-dogged Moon." He saw the "Light of the Compass & rudderman's Lamp reflected with forms on the Main Sail" (*NB*, II, 2001), which anticipates the line "The steersman's face by his lamp gleamed white," also added to later versions. Both of these observations were incorporated into the text in a notebook entry that consisted of a revision of lines 199–204 of the 1798 edition:

With never a whisper on the main
Off shot the spectre ship:
And stifled words & groans of pain

Mix'd on each murmuring lip /
And We look'd round & we look'd up
And Fear at our hearts as at a Cup
  The Life-blood seem'd to sip
The sky was dull & dark the Night,
The Helmsman's Face by his lamp gleam'd bright,
  From the Sails the Dews did drip /
Till clomb above the Eastern Bar
The horned moon, with one bright Star
  Within its nether Tip.
One after one, by the star-dogg'd moon,

&c—

[*NB*, II, 2880]

Coburn is uncertain about the exact date of this revision but suggests that it might be late fall 1806 or early 1807. Thus at least by this time he was working on revisions that did not appear until 1817, and the insights Coleridge records in his notebooks until then may be used to study what he knew about the mariner's nightmare. Interestingly enough, most of the important additions to the poem after 1798, exclusive of the gloss, contain significant clarifications of his understanding of the nightmare.[5]

Also on the voyage to Malta, when he was free from the tyranny of emotional disturbances but still seasick in his cabin, he imagined what a death by drowning would be like:

Sleeps, these Horrors, these frightful Dreams of Despair when the sense of individual Existence is full & lively only for one to feel oneself powerless, crushed *in* by every power—a stifled boding, one abject miserable Wretch / yet hopeless, yet struggling, removed from all touch of Life, deprived of all notion of Death / strange mixture of Fear and Despair—& that passio purissima, that mere Passiveness with Pain (the essence of which is perhaps Passivity—& which our word—mere Suffering—well comprizes—) in which the Devils are the Antithesis of Deity, who is Actus Purissimus, and eternal Life, as they are an ever-living Death.

[*NB*, II, 2078]

The phrase "an ever-living Death" was later reworded as the "Nightmare Life-in-Death," which was also a later addition to the poem. The terms he used to describe death by water are those he commonly

[5]In the 1834 text these are lines 41–50, 143–46, 187–89, 193–94, and 203–8, all of which have to do specifically with the nightmare. I will comment upon these in the course of my argument. For the view that opium dreams after 1800 influenced these revisions, see R. C. Bald's discussion of several of these lines in his "Coleridge and *The Ancient Mariner:* Addenda to *The Road to Xanadu,*" in *Nineteenth-Century Studies,* ed. Herbert Davis et al. (Ithaca, N.Y.: Cornell Univ. Press, 1940), pp. 1–45.

used to describe the nightmare, in which one of the consistent symptoms is suffocation. Powerless in such a nightmare, he was unable to act at all and merely suffered. The implications of this entry for his struggle to account for the mystery of moral evil and the tentative answer he offers are significant.

Even before the writing of the first text of the poem, nightmares and various degrees of mental derangement fascinated him. He was well aware of his own tendency to isolate himself from the ordinary referents of sensation. In 1796 Charles Lloyd was living with the Coleridges and was ill much of the time. Coleridge wrote that Lloyd was the victim of "a kind of Night-mair." Lloyd was awake and aware of what occurred around him: "all the Realities round him mingle with, and form a part of, the strange Dream. All his voluntary powers are suspended; but he perceives every thing & hears every thing, and whatever he perceives & hears he perverts into the substance of his delirious Vision" (*CL,* I, 257). Lloyd was suffering from the same diminished sense of reality from which Coleridge suffered. The vividness and permanence of impressions, that check of the senses, were not strong enough to stabilize his mind, and yet the sensations did exist; they were simply not able to counteract the delirium.

The things that are seen in the nightmare might be connected with a sensation from the stomach, and the pain in the internal organs could be interpreted as coming from an external source: "The mind . . . at all times, with and without our distinct consciousness, seeks for and assumes some outward cause for every impression from without, and . . . in sleep by aid of the imaginative faculty converts its judgements respecting the cause into a present image, as being the cause" (*SC,* I, 202). Pains in the stomach, for instance, are represented by an assassin's stabbing one in the side or by a goblin pressing down on the body, as in the paintings of Henry Fuseli, which Coleridge knew.[6] In March 1805 he described one of his own nightmares "which awoke me, & which . . . gave the *idea* and *sensation* of actual grasp or touch contrary to *my* will, & in apparent consequence of the malignant will

[6]Coleridge knew of Fuseli as early as December 1794 and wrote to Southey: "Would not this be a fine subject for a *wild* Ode—

St. Withold footed thrice the Oulds—
He met the Night Mare & her nine Foals—
He bade her alight and her troth plight—
And 'aroynt thee, Witch [']—he said!—

I shall set about one, when I am in a Humor to *abandon* myself to all the Diableries, that ever met the Eye of a Fuseli!" (*CL,* I, 135). Coleridge adapts Edgar's song in *King Lear* (III.iv.125–29).

of the external Form" (*NB*, II, 2468). The forms generated in the nightmare by the imagination usurp the place of an external reality but still borrow vividness from the actual impressions that are combined with them. These abortive creations possess their substantiality because they are believed to possess outness and because they seem independent of the will.

Coleridge was careful to distinguish between a dream and a nightmare. The dream occurs during sleep, but the nightmare occurs most often in the interval between sleep and waking, when all the faculties are awake but operating imperfectly. During a nightmare the imagination, the "true inward creatrix," creates its own forms, and these forms seem real because the reason, "in good measure awake, most generally presents to us all the accompanying images very nearly as they existed the moment before. . . . In short, the nightmare is not, properly, a dream, but a species of reverie, akin to somnambulism, during which the understanding and moral sense are awake, though more or less confused, and over the terrors of which the reason can exert no influence."[7]

For the second edition of *Lyrical Ballads* Coleridge, doubtless under the pressure of Wordsworth's critical apology for the poem, subtitled the poem "A Poet's Reverie," a title against which Lamb vehemently protested. Wordsworth himself had used *reverie* in "The Reverie of Poor Susan," and both Coleridge and Wordsworth may have known Darwin's definition of it in *Zoonomia*. Darwin described a reverie as a state in which we are not conscious of time and place while we pursue "some interesting train of ideas" and while we "do not distinguish this train of sensitive and voluntary ideas from the irritative ones excited by the presence of external objects, though our organs of sense are surrounded with their accustomed stimuli."[8] But Coleridge characteristically modified the usage of the word. Darwin stipulated that reverie was a willed pursuit of ideas; Coleridge knew that the reverie and the nightmare were products of a weakened will.

In the nightmare the imagination is not a visionary faculty which perceives a harmonious order that exists independently of the mind; rather, its creations are determined solely by a particular derangement in which normal perceptions are distorted by fear and terror.

[7] *Anima Poetae*, ed. E. H. Coleridge (Boston: Houghton Mifflin, 1895), pp. 206–7. The original is in Notebook 18 and is dated Jan. 29, 1811, prior to the 1817 text of "The Ancient Mariner." Coleridge's distinction between dreams and nightmares has been in part verified by modern sleep research. See Charles Fisher et al., "A Psychophysiological Study of Nightmares," *Journal of the American Psychoanalytic Association*, 18 (1970), 747–82.

[8] Erasmus Darwin, *Zoonomia; or, The Laws of Organic Life* (Dublin, 1800), I, 260.

Coleridge was most familiar with his imagination as a power that was creative and active, even in the years after "Dejection," in which he lamented the loss of his "shaping spirit." That spirit never left him completely, and it was never a question to him whether his mind was able to create its own forms from the materials presented to it. The significant question was whether the imagination could be controlled by the reason and the senses. Unfortunately for his peace of mind, too often his diseased imagination exposed his fears and feelings of guilt, and the greater the vividness of his creations, the greater his conviction that they were substantial realities.

Whatever we see of the mariner's world we see through the mariner's eyes. He does not comprehend what happens to him, but our view of him is Coleridge's, and what Coleridge conveys is the knowledge of the mariner's modes of perception. From both the mariner's point of view and ours, it is difficult to follow any clear pattern of crime and punishment. Robert Penn Warren's essay, in spite of its controversial statements on symbolism and allegory, still remains the most influential exposition of this view. The mariner's self-assertive, satanic will commits a crime against the order of the universe, the One Life, and the mariner must therefore undergo the trials of spiritual desiccation until the imagination can restore the connection between his soul and the One Life. Warren cites *The Statesman's Manual* to explain the evil of the mariner's killing the albatross: "in its utmost abstraction and consequent state of reprobation, the will becomes Satanic pride and rebellious self-idolatry in the relations of the spirit to itself, and remorseless despotism relatively to others . . . by the fearful resolve to find in itself alone the one absolute motive of action."[9]

There are, however, a number of difficulties with a reading that sees a traditional pattern of crime and punishment. The mariner himself believes, as Edward Bostetter points out, that his fate is determined by the whim of a tyrannous God.[10] More importantly, the mariner feels persecuted even before he kills the albatross, the ostensible reason for his being punished in the first place. If the killing of the bird were a crime for which he is punished, guilt and persecution would occur only after the killing of the bird. The storm that drives the ship to the pole is personified as a pursuing demon. The mariner does not feel himself part of a One Life or a world governed by a benevolent deity. He simply finds himself in a capricious and unreasoning world and feels persecuted before he commits any overt act

[9] Warren, p. 228. Warren quotes from *Aids to Reflection,* in *Works,* I, 458.
[10] Bostetter, pp. 244–45.

which could reasonably be expected to bring persecution upon him. The fear that chills his life's blood when he sees the death ship is present before the albatross arrives.

Driven by a north wind to the pole, the ship is becalmed in the ice and snow before the albatross arrives bringing, as the crew believes, the south wind. In the calm at the pole there is wonder mixed with fear of the unknown. The noise of the cracking ice reaches the mariner's ears "like noises of a swound." The phrase "of a swound" made no sense to readers in 1798, and Coleridge removed it from the 1800 edition and inserted "A wild and ceaseless sound." Later he altered the original line by substituting the word *in* for *of* and restored the original line in subsequent editions. Lowes indicates that the line "in a swound" refers not merely to a swoon or fainting fit, but to "the gates of consciousness as one emerges from a swoon," "that limbo of alien terror and unearthly detachment from reality" when one is aware of the supernatural.[11] Lowes's gloss suggests that Coleridge was referring directly to that transition point where the consciousness is regaining its contact with reality yet is still in the nightmare. Thus the alteration of "of a swound" to "in a swound" takes the reader more directly into the sensations experienced by the sailors before the albatross arrives. The revised lines are further evidence for saying that after 1800 Coleridge came to understand the mariner's condition. With the arrival of the storm the mariner has already begun to slide into the nightmare.

The inclusion of the killing of the albatross as a specific reason for the mariner's suffering was, of course, Wordsworth's idea. "Suppose," Wordsworth reported he said to Coleridge, "you represent him as having killed one of these birds on entering the South Sea, and that the tutelary spirits of these regions take upon them to avenge the crime."[12] In the first edition Coleridge does little more than report that the mariner killed the bird. The addition of the gloss does not illuminate the reasons, if there were conscious reasons, for the act. It may help to determine the consequences of the act, but it does little to determine the cause. Coleridge did provide a hint in his revisions of the lines on the storm. The single stanza of 1798,

> Listen, Stranger! Storm and Wind,
> A Wind and Tempest strong!
> For days and weeks it play'd us freaks—
> Like Chaff we drove along.
>
> [1798; ll. 45–48]

[11] Lowes, pp. 147–48.

[12] Christopher Wordsworth, *Memoirs of William Wordsworth* (London: Moxon, 1851), I, 107.

was expanded to two stanzas later:

> And now the STORM-BLAST came, and he
> Was tyrannous and strong:
> He struck with his o'ertaking wings,
> And chased us south along.
>
> With sloping masts and dipping prow,
> As who pursued with yell and blow
> Still treads the shadow of his foe,
> And forward bends his head,
> The ship drove fast, loud roared the blast,
> And southward aye we fled.
>
> [ll. 41–50]

In the first version, the storm is a naturalistic one that drives the ship before it, but in later editions it is personified as a pursuing bird. An impersonal and irrational storm became a demon in purposeful pursuit of the crew and particularly of the mariner. The force that had to be endured by all mariners as a matter of course became persecution of the mariner himself. Terrorized by the storm's personal attack and confused by the unearthly noises of the swound, the mariner unconsciously associates the albatross with the storm while he and the crew outwardly receive the bird as a member of their Christian community.

The wedding guest also may make the same association between the storm and the bird. When the mariner's countenance changes just before his confession of having killed the bird, the wedding guest says, "God save thee, ancient Mariner! / From the fiends, that plague thee thus!" Why should he express fear when the mariner has been talking of the albatross, which was welcomed with Christian hospitality? The reference of the plural "fiends" is certainly to the storm, perhaps also the ambiguous "Nor shapes of men nor beasts we ken" and the albatross itself. Similarly, the crew may connect the albatross and the storm. After the albatross is killed, they blame the mariner for killing the spirit that brought the wind. Of course, at that moment, the wind was not a pursuing demon or storm but a method of escape from the calm at the pole; nevertheless, in their imperfect understanding, the association is made.

Coleridge himself realized that the search for a specific motive for a particular action was futile. In a contribution to Southey's *Omniana,* he wrote that "it is a matter of infinite difficulty, but fortunately of comparative indifference to determine what a man's motive may have been for this or that particular action. Rather seek to learn what his objects in general are. What does he habitually wish, habitually pursue? and thence deduce his impulses which are commonly the true efficient causes of men's conduct; and without which the motive itself would not have become a motive" (*LR,* I, 297). He knew that the common condition of mankind, the disposition to commit evil acts, could be represented by a man's habitual actions, but its ultimate origin could not be represented by one act such as the eating of an apple or the killing of a bird. The origin of man's inclination to evil is prior to its temporal manifestations.[13]

Until the blessing of the watersnakes at the end of Part IV, the course of the mariner's nightmare carries him further and further within himself and away from exterior reality. The killing of the albatross is one step, but not the first, in a series of actions in the isolation of the mind from the check of the senses. It is paradoxically a striking out against the bird and a turning away from it in fear. The sequence of events begins with the unveiling of his fear, his habitual response to things he cannot understand.

In the midst of the unfamiliar antarctic landscape of ice and snow, of strange lights reflected by and through the ice, of strange forms of life, the albatross is the one familiar sight. Visually it provides the one remaining point upon which the eye can focus and with which the crew is familiar. The mariner's imagination has begun its wanderings, and the killing of the bird removes it from the realm of the substantial and transforms it into a symbol of the nightmare world when it is hung around his neck as an outward sign of the curse uttered by the crew. In April 1805 Coleridge was musing on the characteristics of dreams and perhaps not consciously thinking of "The Ancient Mariner," but his speculations have a bearing on the nightmare in the poem. Writing of moments when he himself descended into the distempered dream, he observed that "all the realities about me lose their natural *healing* powers" (*NB,* II, 2557). Less than two weeks previously he had thought about the distinction between the flow of associations in sleep and daydreams and the stabilizing external realities, which he called "outward Forms and Sounds, the Sanctifiers, the Strengtheners" (*NB,* II, 2543). The albatross is a sanctifier in virtue of its being the one recognizable reality in the unfamiliar world.

[13]Coleridge distinguished, in his later prose, between Original Sin and Adam's Fall. The Fall was "successive moments of phenomenal sin . . . that is, of sin as it reveals itself in time, and is an immediate object of consciousness" (*Works,* I, 269n). For a further discussion on these issues in Coleridge's later thought, see James Boulger, *Coleridge as Religious Thinker* (New Haven: Yale Univ. Press, 1961), pp. 158–59; J. A. Stuart, "The Augustinian 'Cause of Action' in Coleridge's *Rime of the Ancient Mariner,*" *Harvard Theological Review,* 60 (1967), 177–211; and J. Robert Barth, S.J., *Coleridge and Christian Doctrine* (Cambridge, Mass.: Harvard Univ. Press, 1969), pp. 114–19.

J. B. Beer believes that the killing of the albatross is existentially right because it symbolizes a rejection of the evidence of the senses which must be transcended to achieve a higher vision.[14] He offers as support for his interpretation a phrase in "The Wanderings of Cain." Cain believes he is punished because he "neglected to make a proper use of his senses" (*PW*, I, 285). The phrase does not necessarily mean that one must reject the senses, and, given the mariner's delirium, it would seem that when one forsakes the familiar world for the freely associating and uncontrolled imagination, nightmare is the unavoidable result.

The mariner's terror deepens with the ship's entrance into the silent sea, a silence that is further proof that there are no external sensations to sustain him and function as sanctifiers. The crew is becalmed at the equator; their physical and mental stasis is a repetition of their lack of motion in the fog and mist at the pole before the south wind arrives to move them toward the equator. But the calm at the equator is a far more horrifying one and marks a deeper and more intense stage in the nightmare. Whereas in the previous calm there had been sounds emanating, at least in part, from the world around them, in this calm there are none at all; the only sound is the mariner's cry. The sun, which in the distorting medium of the fog had risen as gloriously as "God's own head," now takes on the appearance of the "bloody Sun." Previous perceptions are being distorted and transformed into objects of the mariner's nightmare. Before the ship was becalmed at the line, "The fair breeze blew, the white foam flew, / The furrow followed free," but later the ship is "As idle as a painted ship / Upon a painted ocean." The transformation of the picture of the ship is not merely one of the change from motion to stillness; it is also a transformation from a real ship that sails on a real sea to one that is seen only as an image. Coleridge's insistence on the verisimilitude of the earlier image of the ship's wake was motivated by his desire to be as literally accurate as possible. In a note in *Sibylline Leaves,* where the line was printed as "The furrow stream'd off free," he said the original line "was the image as seen by a spectator from the shore, or from another vessel. From the ship itself, the *Wake* appears like a brook flowing off from the stern" (*PW,* I, 190). Changing the image to a more realistic one makes more striking the contrast between the visual reality of being on the ship and participating in its motion and the image seen in the mind's eye.

A further rapid transformation of the image of the ship brings into focus the death ship that arrives shortly afterward. The planks of the

[14] Beer, p. 150.

mariner's ship, warped and dried in the sun, anticipate the naked ribs of the specter ship that transports the Night-mare Life-in-Death. If there is one common emotion in all these perceptions and transformations, it is fear. Fear, as the associating principle, gradually emerges in the mariner's consciousness until at the moment of his seeing the woman he recognizes that fear is destroying him. The lines "Fear at my heart, as at a cup, / My life-blood seemed to sip!" were added to the 1817 text, an addition Coleridge was enabled to make from the observation of his own mental processes. The Hartleyean theories of association, to which Coleridge was earlier attracted, that ideas were brought into the mind by association with other ideas, were rejected because he had learned that the role of feeling was central. In August 1803 he wrote to Southey: "I almost think, that Ideas *never* recall Ideas, as far as they are Ideas—any more than Leaves in a forest create each other's motion—The Breeze it is that runs thro' them / it is the Soul, the state of Feeling."[15]

A few months earlier in 1803, Coleridge was meditating on the feeling of falling asleep: "Contact—the womb—the amnion liquor—warmth + touch / —air cold + touch + sensation & action of breathing—contact of the mother's knees + all those contacts of the Breast + taste & wet & sense of swallowing—Sense of diminished Contact explains the falling asleep— / this *is* Fear, and this produces Fear—" (*NB*, I, 1414). Fear is thus specifically equated with the loss of support and a diminished sensation of touch, in this case of support and love of the mother. It represents a falling away from the security of a natural state of protection. The separation from a natural state here may lend some credence to those who maintain that the traumatic anxieties of childhood may have determined his adult fear and guilt, but at any rate he is fully conscious of the connection between fear and the loss of support. Fear is being literally out of touch with reality and is an essential part of the nightmare. The mariner falls away from reality and in doing so kills the symbol of community and outness that eventually results in his separation from the crew. The

[15] *CL*, II, 961. This statement may have originated with Dr. Beddoes's statement that "feelings that have accompanied ideas at different times, have prodigious power in bringing these ideas together; and this is the chief secret for unriddling the inconsistencies of dreams, and the key to the boldest flights of lyric and dithyrambic poetry." To his observation Beddoes appends this note: "I only touch here on the associating power of the feelings. It is the most neglected, and perhaps at the same time the most pregnant topic in the doctrine of the mind" (*Hygëia* [Bristol, 1803], III, 90). Although Coleridge disliked the essay on mania (the statement quoted above is not in that essay), he thought the rest of *Hygëia* a "valuable & useful work" (*CL*, II, 937).

plural "we" used prior to his shooting the bird becomes the lonely "I" for the rest of the voyage. He is in the state of the bound Prometheus in which, as Northrop Frye explains, "fear is primary." And for fear "the obvious complementary symbol is that of the coy, teasing, elusive *femme fatale.*"[16]

The crew represent a potential alternative to the mariner's withdrawing into himself in fear. Having forsworn responsibility for the crime they condoned, they share his fear, but their fear turns to anger and superstition. In the *Biographia* Coleridge wrote that "in all perplexity there is a portion of fear, which predisposes the mind to anger" (*BL,* I, 52), and anger is characteristic of men "whose dearest wishes are fixed on objects wholly out of their own power" (*BL,* I, 25). The members of the crew are victims of superstition, which Coleridge saw as a "debility and dimness of the imaginative power, and a consequent necessity of reliance on the immediate impressions of the senses" (*BL,* I, 19). For a short period they share the mariner's fate because they share his basic fear; they too are victimized by the storm, and like the mariner they feel persecuted. But instead of withdrawing into themselves as the mariner does they find external causes for their distress:

And I had done a hellish thing,
And it would work 'em woe:
For all averred, I had killed the bird
That made the breeze to blow.
Ah wretch! said they, the bird to slay,
That made the breeze to blow!

Nor dim nor red, like God's own head,
The glorious Sun uprist:
Then all averred, I had killed the bird
That brought the fog and mist.
'Twas right, said they, such birds to slay,
That bring the fog and mist.

. . . . .

Ah! well a-day! what evil looks
Had I from old and young!
Instead of the cross, the Albatross
About my neck was hung.

[ll. 91–102, 139–42]

[16]Northrop Frye, *A Study of English Romanticism* (New York: Random House, 1968), p. 113. Bostetter prints an interesting definition from Coleridge's MS essay "On the Passions": fear is a "combination of *Impulse* and *Seizure*" ("Coleridge's Manuscript Essay 'On the Passions,'" *JHI,* 31 [1970], 101). Freud defines anxiety as a "percep-

The mariner understands no more of their fate than he does of his own. He sees their death, as he sees his own submission to the Night-mare Life-in-Death, determined by the roll of dice. The ultimate judgment upon their souls seems to have nothing to do with their opinions, superstitions, or acts of condoning and then cursing the mariner's actions. After the departure of the death ship the men die: "The souls did from their bodies fly,— / They fled to bliss or woe!" Thus their souls' final abode is either heaven or hell—the mariner cannot judge.

When the mariner spies the speck on the horizon, he hails it expecting that it will bring relief to him and the crew, but when it turns into the specter ship, his nightmare is completed. He turns his eyes away from the horrors he sees, and the other sailors die one by one under the "star-dogg'd Moon." In the margin of a copy of the poem, Coleridge wrote that "it is a common superstition among sailors that something evil is about to happen whenever a star dogs the moon" (*NB,* II, 2880n). The crew's fear turns to anger against the mariner, and having become the object of the crew's anger, the mariner cannot choose the alternative of the crew. He consistently sees himself accused and persecuted.

The Night-mare Life-in-Death arises in his consciousness and completely overwhelms him. His senses are dulled to the point of being inoperative: "Each throat / Was parched, and glazed each eye" (ll. 143–44). The vision of the death ship then gradually grows in his eyes:

> At first it seemed a little speck,
> And then it seemed a mist;
> It moved and moved, and took at last
> A certain shape, I wist.
>
> A speck, a mist, a shape, I wist!
> And still it neared and neared:
> As if it dodged a water-sprite,
> It plunged and tacked and veered.
>
> [ll. 149–56]

Here there is no sensation from the exterior world; the images of the mind have completely replaced sensation, and the fear that was perhaps only semiconscious at the killing of the albatross becomes chillingly clear. If in Coleridge's later writings on the nightmare he con-

---

tion of the absence of an object" and "'primal anxiety' of birth" as "separation from the mother" (*The Problem of Anxiety,* trans. Henry Alden Bunker [New York: Psychoanalytic Press and W. W. Norton, 1936], p. 76).

sistently mentions that nightmare takes place when sensation is present but distorted, here the mariner sinks beneath the nightmare, a state destructive to his entire personality.

At first the mariner thinks that what he sees will provide him with some form of release:

> With throats unslaked, with black lips baked,
> We could nor laugh nor wail;
> Through utter drought all dumb we stood!
> I bit my arm, I sucked the blood,
> And cried, A sail! a sail!
>
> With throats unslaked, with black lips baked,
> Agape they heard me call:
> Gramercy! they for joy did grin,
> And all at once their breath drew in,
> As they were drinking all.
>
> [ll. 157–66]

The normal cause-and-effect relationships and the customary sensations are replaced by a world that astounds the mariner by its capriciousness. The ship approaches without breeze and without tacking and takes its place in front of the setting sun. The only significant action the mariner deliberately takes becomes a "dear ransom," and only more horror follows. The sucking of his own blood, a further turning inward, represents a desire for release from his torment in any way possible.

"The Wanderings of Cain," written at the same time as "The Ancient Mariner," contains an interesting gloss on the biting of the arm. At the end of the second canto, Cain is told by the shape of his murdered brother that in killing him Cain had removed Abel from the dominion of the God of the living and hurled him into the land of the God of the dead. Consumed by his burning agony, Cain feels the curse of God upon him, and desiring death, he asks, "Who is the God of the dead? where doth he make his dwelling? what sacrifices are acceptable unto him?" (*PW*, I, 292). The shape of Abel bids Cain to follow him, but the fragment breaks off. In another version there is a further elaboration of the sacrifice. A devil in the guise of Abel appears to Cain and bids him to "offer sacrifice, for himself and his son Enoch by cutting his child's arm and letting the blood fall from it" (*PW*, I, 286). The mariner's biting his arm may also be a wish for any release, even death.

The "dear ransom" is a sacrifice of his life's blood for the power of speech that allows him to call for what he thinks will be a rescue. But it is certainly a perversion of a salvation through a Eucharist, because the mariner does not possess the strength and purity to make his sacrifice into a salvation for the crew. The ransom becomes a suicide. Instead of salvation, the death ship arrives, and after it departs the mariner is frozen in fear. The Night-mare Life-in-Death is a vampire who sucks the mariner's blood; she is the objectification of his fear and symbolically repeats his action of sucking the blood.

Part IV finds the mariner "alone on a wide wide sea," completely isolated from every living thing. Whereas before the arrival of the death ship the mariner could look upon the exterior world even though he saw it as a dead thing, now he cannot bear to look outside himself:

> I looked upon the rotting sea,
> And drew my eyes away;
> I looked upon the rotting deck,
> And there the dead men lay.
>
> I looked to heaven, and tried to pray;
> But or ever a prayer had gusht,
> A wicked whisper came, and made
> My heart as dry as dust.
>
> I closed my lids, and kept them close,
> And the balls like pulses beat;
> For the sky and the sea, and the sea and sky
> Lay like a load on my weary eye,
> And the dead were at my feet.
>
> [ll. 240–52]

Just before the ship arrived his eyes had been "glazed," his senses disturbed, but now he cannot even look beyond himself because he fears that he will see only a reflection of his own misery. Gradually he has retreated from the stabilizing reality of sensation. During this retreat, thoughtless as it may have appeared at first, the nightmare usurps the place of reality. Up to this point the habitual impulse of the mariner has been to withdraw into himself.

Throughout the mariner's retreat he bears the burden of the paralyzing conviction of his own guilt. The questions of moral evil and personal guilt were frequently on Coleridge's mind. The well-known entry in the Gutch Memorandum Book, "The Origin of Evil, an Epic Poem," (*NB,* I, 161), is only one of the indications that the subject was on his mind. In a letter of February 11, 1797, Lamb urged Coleridge to finish the poems he had spoken of on his previous visit to London, among them one on the origin of evil.[17] Coleridge confessed to his brother George, who had become suspicious of his unpredictable brother's radical opinions on the perfectibility of man,

[17] *Letters of Charles and Mary Lamb,* ed. E. V. Lucas (London: Dent, 1935), I, 95.

that he believed "most stedfastly in original Sin" (*CL,* I, 396). "The Ancient Mariner" itself was written, Coleridge tells us in a note to "The Wanderings of Cain," when he and Wordsworth had jointly attempted to write a poem on the sins of Cain and their expiation. None of Coleridge's discussions of the origin of moral evil made before the first edition of "The Ancient Mariner" are directly applicable to the poem. But during the period of 1803–06, that period when he was making some of the most important revisions, there are several notebook entries having a direct bearing on the problems in the poem. In October 1803, during one of his attempts to free himself from the opium habit and the domestic and physical ills that occasioned the addiction, he began one of his most prolonged dialogues with himself on the nature of evil. He had just returned from a walking tour of Scotland with William and Dorothy Wordsworth, a month in which he was consistently plagued by illness and distempered dreams. The tour had produced "The Pains of Sleep," the only poem written that year:

But yester-night I prayed aloud
In anguish and in agony,
Up-starting from the fiendish crowd
Of shapes and thoughts that tortured me:
A lurid light, a trampling throng,
Sense of intolerable wrong,
And whom I scorned, those only strong!
Thirst of revenge, the powerless will
Still baffled, and yet burning still!
Desire with loathing strangely mixed
On wild or hateful objects fixed.
Fantastic passions! maddening brawl!
And shame and terror over all!
Deeds to be hid which were not hid,
Which all confused I could not know
Whether I suffered, or I did:
For all seemed guilt, remorse or woe,
My own or others still the same
Life-stifling fear, soul-stifling shame.

[ll. 14–32]

The artistic control and objectivity Coleridge was able to maintain in "The Ancient Mariner" are gone, and a more direct confessional mode replaces them. Nevertheless, the fears of a horrible guilt, the uncertainty as to whether he is a victim merely suffering or an active agent of evil, the petrifying and stifling effects of the fiendish nightmare figures are reminiscent of the mariner's visions.

On the twenty-seventh of October he engaged in an argument with

Hazlitt, who was then painting his portrait, about the origin of moral evil. Afterwards, Coleridge wrote in the privacy of his notebook that he had solved "the whole business of the Origin of Evil satisfactorily to my own mind." Hazlitt had challenged him with the question as to why an infinitely good God had created evil, and privately Coleridge rephrased the question: "why, in short, did not the Almighty create an absolutely infinite number of Almighties?" (*NB*, I, 1619). Coleridge's answer to this impious question is that "there is in the essence of the divine nature a necessity of omniform harmonious action, and that Order, & System / not number—in itself base & disorderly & irrational— / define the creative Energy" (*NB*, I, 1622). Coleridge's refutation reflects his conviction that it is erroneous to conceive of the world as based on the mere addition of number to number.

Satisfying as this solution might be for a metaphysician, it was too abstract to account for his own feelings of shame and guilt. In December he returned to the question with what may have been a new insight into the problem:

> I will at least make the attempt to explain to myself the Origin of moral Evil from the *streamy* Nature of Association, which Thinking = Reason, curbs & rudders / how this comes to be so difficult / Do not the bad Passions in Dreams throw light & shew of proof upon this Hypothesis?—Explain those bad Passions: & I shall gain Light, I am sure—A Clue! A Clue!—an Hecatomb a la Pythagoras, if it unlabyrinths me.

Predictably, it did not unlabyrinth him immediately, for he wrote this passage late in the evening of the twenty-eighth, and in the early hours of the next morning he thought of the

> blessedness of Innocent Children, the blessedness of sweet Sleep, &c &c &c: are these or are they not contradictions to the evil from *streamy* association?—I hope not: all is to be thought *over* and *into*—but what is the height, & ideal of mere association?—Delirium.—But how far is this state produced by Pain & Denaturalization? And what are these?—In short, as far as I can see any thing in this Total Mist, Vice is imperfect yet existing Volition, giving diseased Currents of association, because it yields on all sides & *yet* is—So think of Madness:—O if I live!
>
> [*NB*, I, 1770]

He is closer to an explanation of the nature of evil as he had witnessed it in his own experience, but he is clearly worried about the theoretical implications, the supposed innocence of children whose minds drift with this flow of association. And if their minds so run, is it evidence of their original sin? At this moment he could not answer these questions, but he seems certain that the flow of "mere association" is a delirium brought on by the diseased powers of volition.

On January 10 of the following year, the problem was still on his mind, and the same solution came to him in a meditation about the pain caused by a sudden interruption of the laws of association. While he was thinking

without any reference to or distinct recollection of my former theory, I saw great Reason to attribute the effect wholly to the streamy nature of the associating Faculty and especially as it is evident that *they most* labor under this defect who are most reverie-ish & streamy—Hartley, for instance & myself / This seems to me no common corroboration of my former Thought on the origin of moral Evil in general.

[*NB*, I, 1833]

The previous labyrinth of speculation had acquired the status of a theory in a few weeks, but he is uncertain about a theory which explained the phenomena with which he was acquainted and yet also seemed to cast doubt on the innocence of children.

A little more than a year later, in April 1805, he returned to this train of thought at a time when he had composed himself and had rigorously halted his tendency to drift into daydream:

So akin to Reason is Reality, that what I could *do* with exulting Innocence, I can not always *imagine* with perfect innocence / for Reason and Reality can stop and stand still, new Influxes from without counteracting the Impulses from within, and *poising* the Thought. But Fancy and Sleep *stream on;* and (instead of outward Forms and Sounds, the Sanctifiers, the Strengtheners!) they connect with them motions of the blood and nerves, and images forced into the mind by the feelings that arise out of the position & state of the Body and its different members. I have done innocently what afterwards in absence I have likewise day-dreamed innocently, during the being awake; but the Reality was followed in Sleep by no suspicious fancies, the Day-dream *has* been. . . .

All the above-going throw lights on my mind with regard to the origin of Evil. **ὑλη** = confusio = passio = finiri—/ / Reason, Action, Forma efformans. (= means "the same as": / / "opposed to".)[18]

He realized that there is an essential evil in daydreams and imaginings and that subjective random trains of association cannot be innocent because the passive mind dissolves into a chaotic phantasmagoria of images and feelings. The active reason, on the other hand, establishes order and restores the ability to act innocently. "*To emancipate itself from the tyranny of association,*" he wrote, "is the most arduous effort of the mind."[19]

[18] *NB*, II, 2543. Coburn untangles the final paragraph as follows: "Matter is the same thing as disorder, which is the same as passivity, which is the same as dissolution [or death], and these are opposed to Reason, Action, self-determinate Form" (*NB*, II, 2543n).

[19] *Friend*, I, 336.

Wordsworth's account of the origin of "The Ancient Mariner" reveals that he understood that the mariner was culpable because the mariner's mind worked the way it did: "some crime was to be committed which should bring upon the Old Navigator, as Coleridge afterwards delighted to call him, the spectral persecution as a consequence of that crime and his own wanderings."[20] As Bernard Blackstone says, "If the wanderings themselves were not criminal, the phrase is meaningless."[21] In the light of Coleridge's notebook entries and, more importantly, of the evidence that we have in the imagery of the poem itself, the phrase must refer to the wanderings of his own diseased and distempered imagination; and it was this general habit of mind more than the single act of the killing of the albatross that plunged the mariner into his delirium.

In "The Ancient Mariner" the will is overwhelmed by the strong currents of fear. The loss of the will, along with the loss of external support, destroys all sense of personal identity. That the mariner has no personality was one of the first points of agreement among Coleridge's friends. Wordsworth complained in the 1800 edition of *Lyrical Ballads* that the mariner "has no distinct character, either in his profession of Mariner, or as a human being who having been long under the controul of supernatural impressions might be supposed himself to partake of something supernatural" (*LB,* p. 277). Lamb was quick to reply that these characteristics were not defects. On January 30, 1801, he complained to Wordsworth: "I totally differ from your idea that the Marinere should have had a character and profession . . . the Ancient Marinere undergoes such Trials, as overwhelm and bury all individuality or memory of what he was, like the state of a man in a Bad dream, one terrible peculiarity of which is: that all consciousness of personality is gone."[22]

Whatever judgment each placed on the mariner's apparent lack of character, both Wordsworth and Lamb agreed on the point that the mariner's personality is destroyed. Specifically, the mariner's will is destroyed, and he is more acted upon than acting. On the voyage to Malta in 1804, Coleridge observed the sailors shooting at a hawk that had been trying to land on the rigging. Finally it was driven off, and he noted that the cruel treatment by the sailors was the result of "non-feeling from non-thinking" (*NB,* II, 2090). Crabb Robinson wrote in his diary that Coleridge had observed that thought "is a laborious breaking through the law of association. The natural train of fancy is violently repressed. The free yielding to its power produces

[20] Christopher Wordsworth, *Memoirs,* I, 107.

[21] *The Lost Travellers* (London: Longmans, 1962), p. 166 n. 1. Blackstone takes the phrase to refer to a mutiny by the crew.

[22] *Letters,* I, 240.

dreaming or delirium" (*MC,* p. 389). The killing of the albatross is thus also a result of a lack of thinking, a destruction of the self from the inability to think about the significance of the act. Humphry House's comment that the mariner's deed is one of a "wicked ignorance because accompanied by a wildly thoughtless failure to consider what might be the truth about the order of the universe"[23] might be modified to say that "wicked ignorance" is an ignorance of the laws of his own mind.

We are now in a better position to judge the relevance of the often-quoted passage from *The Statesman's Manual* which explains that the origin of evil is in the will:

> In its utmost abstraction and consequent state of reprobation, the will becomes Satanic pride and rebellious self-idolatry in the relations of the spirit to itself, and remorseless despotism relatively to others . . . in short, by the fearful resolve to find in itself alone the one absolute motive of action, under which all other motives from within and from without must be either subordinated or crushed.[24]

It is clear that the mariner does not possess anything like a "Satanic pride"; in fact he possesses no will at all, no self and no personality. His sin resides in the will, but it is not rebellion in any traditional sense. Shortly after finishing "The Ancient Mariner," Coleridge wrote to his brother George that he believed "that from our mothers' wombs our understandings are darkened; and even where our understandings are in the Light, that our organization is depraved, & our volitions imperfect" (*CL,* I, 396). The mariner's guilt lies in his inability to organize the mind and the sensations that are presented to it.

After these insights recorded in the notebooks, Coleridge never again allowed his imagination free reign. He was unwilling to open again the Pandora's box of his own mind and free the nightmares and specters that had previously haunted him. Feelings too strong gave him infinite pain. In one of his articles of "confession of belief, with respect to the true grounds of Christian morality," he wrote, "I reject as erroneous, and deprecate as *most* dangerous, the notion that our *feelings* are to be the ground of our actions. I believe the feelings themselves to be among the things that are to be grounded and guided."[25]

[23] House, p. 98.

[24] *Works,* I, 458.

[25] Gillman, p. 359. Perhaps more well-known passages in which Coleridge speaks of the relation of feelings to philosophy and theology should be read in the light of this statement of belief. See particularly *CL,* I, 279: "My philosophical opinions are

The tentative questionings in the notebooks and the concrete experience of the poems indicated a theory that located the origin of evil in the mind's inability to control itself, but each time he thought of this theory he also thought of his son Hartley and the "blessedness of Innocent Children." Hartley had been used in "Frost at Midnight" and "The Nightingale" as a symbol of the joyous innocent who was not conscious of himself as a person separated from nature. Coleridge found himself at a dead end; both evil and innocence seemed to reside in the same mental activity. He could not extricate himself from this quagmire. D. W. Harding has called attention to the strange mixture of innocence and guilt in "The Ancient Mariner" and to the parallel problem in "The Pains of Sleep."[26] There, as in "The Ancient Mariner," a conviction of guilt coexists with astonishment that he could be mortally punished for a trivial crime or no crime at all. In "The Pains of Sleep" the visitations of terrible dreams clearly confused him:

Such punishments, I said, were due
To natures deepliest stained with sin,—
For aye entempesting anew
The unfathomable hell within,
The horror of their deeds to view,
To know and loathe, yet wish and do!
Such griefs with such men well agree,
But wherefore, wherefore fall on me?

[ll. 43–50]

By the standards of the waking world, the mariner's crime was not a serious one; yet he retains a deep sense of imperfectly understood guilt. Coleridge's early confusion on the problem of evil is reflected in the mariner's bewilderment over the events that happen to him. The fear that rises up in the mariner's nightmare comes in part from his lack of comprehension of the things that are essentially beyond his comprehension. Thus he fears everything, and his anxiety immobilizes his will.

Coleridge's intuitions into the nature of evil and innocence have a direct bearing on the concluding sections of "The Ancient Mariner." The poem has been read as a parable, not only of the Fall, but also of rebirth and redemption. The blessing of the watersnakes is most often

---

blended with, or deduced from, my feelings: & this, I think, peculiarizes my style of Writing"; and *NB,* I, 989: "I do not wish you to act from these truths—no! still & always act from your *feelings.*—but only meditate often on these Truths, that some time or other they may become your Feelings."

26 "The Theme of 'The Ancient Mariner,'" *Scrutiny,* 9 (1941), 334–42.

cited as the single most important event in the redemptive process. The moon rises over the sea, the mariner gazes out at the snakes, and, admiring their beauty, blesses them, and the rains come after his refreshing sleep. He is able to effect a partial restoration of his sense of security. The spontaneous blessing of the watersnakes reverses the increasing introspection of his nightmare, turns his mind to the natural world beyond him, and temporarily suspends his agonized fear. Warren, among many other readers of the poem, sees as the result of the mariner's recognition of the earth's beauty and his act of love a "freedom from the spell."[27] But the reference to a spell is at best ambiguous. The albatross, which had been hung around his neck as a mark of Cain, falls from him, but this single event does not represent a liberation from either the curse of killing the bird or from the curse of Life-in-Death, which he is fated to endure.

The blessing of the snakes reverses only the habitual tendency to retire into himself, is only a symptom of a deeper weakness of his will, and does not repair that fatal weakness that brings the curses upon him in the first place. Just before the ship reaches its home port the mariner awakens from a trance:

> All stood together on the deck,
> For a charnel-dungeon fitter:
> All fixed on me their stony eyes,
> That in the Moon did glitter.
>
> The pang, the curse, with which they died,
> Had never passed away:
> I could not draw my eyes from theirs,
> Nor turn them up to pray.
>
> [ll. 434–41]

When the mariner sees the pilot and the hermit come out to greet the ship, he hopes that the hermit will shrieve him:

> I saw a third—I heard his voice:
> It is the Hermit good!
> He singeth loud his godly hymns
> That he makes in the wood.
> He'll shrieve my soul, he'll wash away
> The Albatross's blood.
>
> [ll. 508–13]

But when the mariner, whose conviction of guilt remains constant, pleads, "O shrieve me, shrieve me, holy man!" (l. 574), the hermit answers, "What manner of man art thou?" The hermit, like the wed-

[27] Warren, p. 244.

ding guest, thinks that the mariner has returned from the dead, and to every character who sees him after the voyage he appears to be a devil. The pilot falls down in a trance, and the pilot's boy goes mad. The mariner, however, takes the question to be a request for confession and to be ultimately about the trials he has undergone and the constitution of his self. Having heard this response from the hermit, the mariner is forced to tell his tale:

> Since then, at an uncertain hour,
> That agony returns:
> And till my ghastly tale is told,
> This heart within me burns.
>
> I pass, like night, from land to land;
> I have strange power of speech;
> That moment that his face I see,
> I know the man that must hear me:
> To him my tale I teach.
> [ll. 582–90]

The necessity of confession as the first step in being shriven is not served by this retelling of the tale. Presumably the story the wedding guest hears has been heard by numerous others transfixed by the mariner's eye, and in this particular relation of the events of the voyage, the mariner reveals no greater understanding of the nature of the specific crime than he possessed before he met the hermit.

By telling the tale, the mariner is forced to relive the entire experience. Coleridge once complained that some engravings showed the mariner "as an old man on board ship. He was in my mind the everlasting wandering Jew—had told this story ten thousand times since the voyage, which was in his early youth and 50 years before."[28] Since confession must contain an understanding of the offense, the original intention of confession is forgotten, and the mariner is never shriven by the hermit.[29] In fact, the mariner becomes the teacher and supplants the hermit as spiritual guide, but his is a posthumous voice. The hermit, like the mariner, is a man apart from society, and like the mariner, is something of a poet: "He singeth loud his godly hymns / That he makes in the wood" (ll. 510–11). His "godly hymns" and his piety are replaced by the mariner's rime, a contrast suggesting that the mariner's ballad comes from a man who, if not eternally cursed, is at least beyond the pale of orthodoxy and cannot be redeemed by the ordinary sacraments of the church.

[28] *NB*, I, 45n. For a discussion of the legend, see George Anderson, *The Legend of the Wandering Jew* (Providence: Brown Univ. Press, 1965).

[29] This point is made by A. M. Buchan, whose reading parallels mine at several points ("The Sad Wisdom of the Mariner," *SP*, 61 [1964], 669–88).

The mariner's inability to confess reflects his lack of comprehension of what has happened to him and his confusion about elementary Christian doctrine, which, as a medieval man, he should know. After the ship reaches the equator, the polar spirit returns southward and the ship is driven home at a speed the mariner cannot endure and so is thrown into a trance. He overhears two spirits discussing his fate, and one says, "The man hath penance done, / And penance more will do" (ll. 408–9), but the mariner's penance is only passive suffering, neither a willed and conscious step toward redemption nor a disciplined spirituality. The penance the mariner hears the spirits speak of can refer only to his agony and nightmare, which are the effects of sin and guilt, or, rather, are the condition of sin, not true penance. Furthermore, he has not yet been shriven, an act consisting of confession and the setting of penance. The voices he hears reflect his own futile attempts to comprehend his fate, one that seems inflicted upon him by mere chance.

The blessing of the watersnakes may temporarily restore the check of the senses and halt the disintegrating flow of the nightmare. For the remainder of the voyage he is as isolated from his senses as he was when he saw the death ship. The more serious deficiency, the abdication of his will, remains. The blessing of the watersnakes itself is an unconscious act:

> A spring of love gushed from my heart,
> And I blessed them unaware:
> Sure my kind saint took pity on me,
> And I blessed them unaware.
>
> [ll. 284–87]

But love was, for Coleridge, always an act of the conscious will: "Love, however sudden, as when we fall in love at first sight . . . is yet an act of the will, and that too one of its primary, and therefore ineffable acts" (*LR,* I, 360). The mariner insists that his love was "unaware"—he no more chose to bless the snakes than he chose to kill the albatross. For the rest of the voyage, moreover, the mariner is as passive as he was before the blessing of the watersnakes. He pulls at the ropes with the inspirited bodies of the crew and takes the oars in the pilot's boat, but these are insignificant actions compared to his inability to confess to the hermit and his being forced to relate his tale by the agony he feels.

The conscious will does not act because it has already died, and the partial restoration comes from the unconscious mind, which was also the source of evil in the first place. As an unconscious act, the blessing of the snakes is an acceptance of the heart's instincts and the source of feelings of both fear and love. The mariner attributes his act of love to the intercession of his "kind saint" and thanks "Mary Queen" for sending sleep into his soul. Characteristically he seeks for a cause for his renewed ability to love in a source outside himself because he does not understand the origins of his passions.

His trip home is marked by a rapid change in emotion, from love and wonder to abject fear, and like his visions in the earlier half of the poem, his visions on the return trip are determined by his feelings. Awakened from the sleep sent into his soul, he feels "that I had died in sleep, / And was a blessѐd ghost" (ll. 307–8). But this joyous mood does not last. The thunderstorm comes, and yet its wind does not move the ship's sails; instead they are moved by the sound of the wind. Images of horror return:

> Beneath the lightning and the Moon
> The dead men gave a groan.
>
> They groaned, they stirred, they all uprose,
> Nor spake, nor moved their eyes;
> It had been strange, even in a dream,
> To have seen those dead men rise.
>
> The helmsman steered, the ship moved on;
> Yet never a breeze up-blew;
> The mariners all 'gan work the ropes,
> Where they were wont to do;
> They raised their limbs like lifeless tools—
> We were a ghastly crew.
>
> [ll. 329–40]

Immediately after the terror of the storm, the dawn brings fresh visions of joy:

> For when it dawned—they dropped their arms,
> And clustered round the mast;
> Sweet sounds rose slowly through their mouths,
> And from their bodies passed.
>
> Around, around, flew each sweet sound,
> Then darted to the Sun;
> Slowly the sounds came back again,
> Now mixed, now one by one.
>
> Sometimes a-dropping from the sky
> I heard the sky-lark sing;
> Sometimes all little birds that are,
> How they seemed to fill the sea and air
> With their sweet jargoning!

And now 'twas like all instruments,
Now like a lonely flute;
And now it is an angel's song,
That makes the heavens be mute.

[ll. 350–66]

This is a second passage often cited as evidence for the mariner's redemption. Warren believes that "in the reanimation of the bodies of the fellow mariners, there is implicit the idea of regeneration and resurrection" and refers to this passage as "this redemption of the sun," asserting that "the Mariner has been redeemed."[30] Although these visions do certainly mark a profound change from the paralyzing fear that gripped the becalmed mariner, he does not respond to such a vision in any way that would convince us that he has indeed been redeemed. The mariner's fate simply cannot be accounted for by traditional Christian teachings on redemption.

It might well be argued that Coleridge himself never intended to present regeneration in terms of orthodox ritual. After all, he resisted these teachings while he was writing the poem, and his personal belief at the time certainly included no such scheme as a medieval Christian would know. Coleridge rejected positions at Norwich and Shrewsbury as a minister just before and while he was writing the poem and explained clearly that he could not administer the sacrament of the Eucharist.[31] He confessed that for his religious opinions on other articles of belief he would "play off my intellect *ad libitum*" (*CL,* I, 366). Instead of traditional Christian doctrine, it might be argued, Coleridge founded the poem upon his reading in Platonic philosophies.

J. B. Beer supports this view, accepting Warren's general thesis that the theme of the poem is the "sacramental vision." The mariner's quest is for the vision of the "inward eye," which he gains when he sees the spirits and sounds circling the sun. Formerly representing the mariner's conscience, the sun has now become the "image of God in human reason." Beer believes that the mariner's voyage is parallel to the Neoplatonic interpretation of Ulysses' voyage in which Ulysses gains the vision of the inward eye and therefore is allowed to return to his own country.[32]

But the mariner arrives in his own country not as one who has understood the mysteries of the universe. His own country is merely

[30] Warren, pp. 245–46.

[31] *CL,* I, 337–38. See also Hazlitt's report that before Coleridge would accept a position, he would preach two sermons, "one on Infant Baptism, the other on the Lord's Supper, shewing that he could not administer either" (Hazlitt, XVIII, 13).

[32] Beer, pp. 150–52, 161–65.

a temporary resting place where the agony of his mental experience first returns to him. He is allowed no repose there but passes "like night, from land to land" constrained to repeat his story.[33] If the inspirited bodies and the circling of the spirits around the sun represent a resurrection and establishment of order in the universe, as both Beer and Warren suggest, clearly the mariner does not participate in it. He stands strangely apart, looking with wonder but without activity, just as Coleridge himself stood aside and did not participate at the center of vision in the Conversation Poems. The mariner emphasizes his distance from the inspirited bodies:

> The body of my brother's son
> Stood by me, knee to knee:
> The body and I pulled at one rope,
> But he said nought to me.
>
> [ll. 341–44]

There is here neither communication with the social, natural world, for it is only the body of the brother's son with whom he works, nor communion with the spiritual one, for there is no beholding of the spirit beside him.

Shortly after being thrown into the trance and hearing the voices proclaim that he has done penance, the mariner awakens during a calm night, and the dead bodies of the crew, still inspirited, fix on him "their stony eyes, / That in the Moon did glitter" (ll. 436–37). His fears and inability to pray return with the reminder that he is still under their curse:

> The pang, the curse, with which they died,
> Had never passed away:
> I could not draw my eyes from theirs,
> Nor turn them up to pray.
>
> And now this spell was snapt: once more
> I viewed the ocean green,
> And looked far forth, yet little saw
> Of what had else been seen—
>
> Like one, that on a lonesome road
> Doth walk in fear and dread,
> And having once turned round walks on,

[33] Bostetter argues that only in the mariner's world is his fate a "partial triumph" and reward because "the best that can be hoped for is the partial redemption from horror, the compensatory power of speech which he is granted" ("The Nightmare World of *The Ancient Mariner,*" p. 251). But the mariner cannot control that power; the tale is told only when the mariner is compelled to tell it by the agony within. He can choose neither to tell it nor to avoid telling it.

And turns no more his head;
Because he knows, a frightful fiend
Doth close behind him tread.

[ll. 438–51]

Surely this is no part of the vision of the mysteries of the universe. The mariner is haunted by his fear of the return of the nightmare, which he knows will always be with him wherever he goes. The return of the curse anticipates its return in the future. The fear he expresses resembles strikingly those he experienced even before the albatross was murdered:

With sloping masts and dipping prow,
As who pursued with yell and blow
Still treads the shadow of his foe,
And forward bends his head. . . .

[ll. 45–48]

The mariner periodically reverts to the feelings of persecution he had at the beginning of the trip; he is unable to conquer the fear even though he has seen visions that might be expected to reveal to him an order in the universe and a vision of the inward eye.

The source of the "lonesome road" passage is Wordsworth's "Salisbury Plain," the first of several versions of the poem that was eventually published as "Guilt and Sorrow."[34] A traveler on the plain has heard supernatural voices and is "mocked as by a hideous dream": "Till then as if his terror dogged his road / He fled, and often backward cast his face" (ll. 127–28). Wordsworth may have brought out these early manuscripts while Coleridge was at work on "The Ancient Mariner," and perhaps Coleridge read some of the drafts. He wrote Cottle to ask him on Wordsworth's behalf if he were interested in publishing the poem (*CL,* I, 400). Not contained in the first draft, "Salisbury Plain," but written at the end of the notebook in which it was copied are the following stanzas that are preliminary steps toward the expanded "Adventures on Salisbury Plain," the next version of the poem, in which the interest shifts from the story of the female vagrant to the sailor who had committed a murder:

[34] The text of "Salisbury Plain" is printed by Stephen Gill, "The Original *Salisbury Plain:* Introduction and Text," in *Bicentenary Wordsworth Studies,* ed. Jonathan Wordsworth (Ithaca, N.Y.: Cornell Univ. Press, 1970), pp. 142–79. All of the texts of "Guilt and Sorrow" will be published as *The Salisbury Plain Poems,* the first volume in the *Cornell Wordsworth.* Wordsworth told Alexander Dyce that he had suggested several stanzas, which he quoted, and "four or five lines more in different places of the poem" (Dyce, p. 185). Could these lines be Wordsworth's?

And little grieved he for the sleety shower,
Cold wind and hunger he had long withstood,
Long hunted down by man's confederate power
Since phrenzy-driven he dipped his hand in blood;
Yet till that hour he had been mild and good;
And when the miserable deed was done
Such pangs were his as to relenting mood
Might melt the hardest [?heart] since has he run
For years from place to place, nor known one cheerful sun.

Yet oft as Fear her withering grasp forbears
Such tendency to pleasures loved before
Does Nature show [ ] common cares
Might to his breast a second spring restore,
The least complaint of wretchedness explore
His inmost heartstrings to responsive tone.
Trembling, the best of human hearts not more,
From each excess of pain his days have known
Well has he learned to make all others ills his own.

Yet though to softest sympathy inclined
Most trivial cause will rouse the heaviest pang
Of terror overwhelm[ing] [ ] his mind
For then with scarce distinguishable clang
In the cold wind a sound of iron rang.
He looked and saw on a bare gibbet nigh
In clanking chains a human body hang
A hovering raven oft did round it fly
A grave the[re] was beneath which he could not descry.

[*WPW*, I, 97–98]

"The Adventures on Salisbury Plain" concludes with the sailor's open confession of guilt and surrender to justice:

Blest be for once the stroke that ends tho' late
The pangs, which from thy halls of terror came
Thou who of Justice bear'st the violated name.

[*WPW*, I, 126]

The execution merely ends his consciousness of his crime. The final lines are truly grim, having no resemblance to the consolations that conclude "Guilt and Sorrow":

They left him hung on high in iron case,
And dissolute men unthinking and untaught,
Planted their festive [?] beneath his face;
And to that spot, which idle numbers sought,
Woman and children were by Fathers brought,

And now some kindred sufferer driven, perchance,
That way, when into storm the sky is wrought,
Upon the swinging corpse his eye may glance
And drop, as he once dropped, in miserable trance.
[*WPW*, I, 127]

The sailor traveling upon the plain is a type of ancient mariner voyaging on the sea. Both are pursued by a tremendous guilt, although Wordsworth insists upon there being a more rational cause for the guilt. Wordsworth's traveler must continue to move and knows "no cheerful sun," just as the mariner is plagued by the "hot and bloody Sun." Most important for the parallel are the second and third stanzas Wordsworth wrote at the end of the notebook that contains "Salisbury Plain." There, fear, which clearly has paralyzed the mariner too, temporarily releases its grasp upon the sailor, and nature restores "to his breast a second spring." Not nature, but the intervention of the "kind saint" allows the mariner his "second spring" when he blesses the watersnakes. For the sailor "though to softest sympathy inclined / Most trivial cause will rouse the heaviest pang / Of terror overwhelming." The slightest reminder of his guilt renders the ministry of nature ineffectual. So great, too, is the mariner's guilt that the blessing of the watersnakes and the vision of the spirits circling the sun cannot permanently expel the persecuting guilt. During his wanderings the sailor sees a body hanging on a gibbet and falls into a trance; so, too, at the end of the poem, do the festive, idle persons who chance upon the spot where the sailor is hanged sink down in "miserable trance" when they see him. The persons "unthinking and untaught" who are stunned into a trance are the forerunners of the wedding guest, who, on the way to attend a marriage festival, is taught by the mariner. In both poems there is a repetition of the experience of guilt in hitherto thoughtless minds.

The "lonesome road" passage also has an interesting connection with Dante's *Inferno*. One of Coleridge's own copies of *Sibylline Leaves*, which after his death passed through the hands of James Gillman and the Watson family, contains next to this passage the penciled notation "From Dante." The handwriting is not Coleridge's but most probably that of someone who was intimate with him in his final years and may well reflect one of Coleridge's own comments. Lowes cites a passage from the Carlyle translation of the *Inferno*, XXI, 25–30, which he believes is closest to the stanza from "The Ancient Mariner":

Then I turned round, like one who longs to see what he must shun, and who is dashed with sudden fear, so that he puts not off his flight to look; and behind us I saw a black Demon come running up the cliff.

Lowes was unable to say that Coleridge knew enough Italian so that one could point to Dante as a source, but whether Coleridge did or did not, either he or someone close to him associated this stanza with the *Inferno*.[35] Taken in conjunction with the evidence from the stanza itself, this underscores the difficulty of reading the homeward journey as a prolonged vision of joy and steps towards redemption.

Finally we might consider the common contention that the blessing of the watersnakes and the vision of the sun signal a return of the powers of the mariner's imagination. The imagination the mariner is said to possess at the end of the voyage is not merely an aesthetic faculty; the claim is made that the mariner is able to transcend the senses and see into the life of things, the world of spirits adumbrated in the epigraph from Burnet. The famous definitions of imagination in the *Biographia* insist, however, that the imagination is always under the control of the conscious will and understanding. Yet something has gone amiss with the soul of the mariner; he has been unable to integrate his faculties and establish a self. Both Lamb and Wordsworth knew that the mariner had lost the possibility of becoming a self on the voyage. There is the unmistakable emphasis throughout that the mariner is more acted upon than acting. When he acts for his betterment, he acts "unawares," and when his state improves to one of joy, his reason beholds but does grasp the phantasmagoria.

Henry Nelson Coleridge's report of Coleridge's conversation with Mrs. Barbauld does not justify our reading the final sections of the poem as a return toward a fully operative imagination. Mrs. Barbauld had complained that "The Ancient Mariner" "had no moral." Coleridge's reply was that it "had too much; and that the only or chief fault, if I might say so, was the obtrusion of the moral sentiment so openly on the reader as a principle or cause of action in work of such pure imagination."[36] This version, printed in *Table Talk* (1835), was preceded by a slightly different version of the conversation recorded in H. N. Coleridge's review of Coleridge's *Poetical Works* in the *Quarterly Review* of August 1834. There he is reported to have said, "In a work of such pure imagination I ought not to have stopped to give reasons for things, or inculcate humanity to beasts."[37] This earlier version does not use the word "imagination" with the full connotations it has in his other published writings. It means merely that the reader is not to apply the standard categories of cause and effect and moral judgment that one might to another kind of work. The em-

[35] Lowes, pp. 525–28.
[36] *Works*, VI, 324.
[37] *Quarterly Review*, 52 (1834), 28.

phasis is upon the negative definition of the poem—what it is not. In both accounts of the conversation the analogy is made between "The Ancient Mariner" and *The Arabian Nights*. For those who are on the prowl for moral sentiment and demand it in serious literature, "The Ancient Mariner" and *The Arabian Nights* should be read in the same spirit. But for those who are not restricted to seeking morality all of a kind, "The Ancient Mariner" possesses a moral far more fundamental than the kind that would be obvious to all.

The difficulties in understanding the final three sections are not due merely to the marvelous mysteries that confuse our ordinary frames of reference. Coleridge's poem cannot be easily placed into a pattern that defines its themes by generalizing its mythical qualities. Perhaps Coleridge was solely interested in the nightmare in the fourth section and used any means to get the mariner back to his native country to complete the voyage. Some support is given for this position by Wordsworth's statement that he suggested that the ship be navigated by the dead crew members.[38] But this point of view flippantly dismisses almost half of what may be the most fascinating poem in the language by a poet who was most concerned with the problems of organic form and the creative process. That he was unwilling to round out a poem by the addition of anything that would merely complete the symmetry is attested by the many fragments that he published.

The problems in reading the final sections come finally from Coleridge's uncertainty about the nature of evil and innocence and the possible means of redemption for someone who has suffered as the mariner does. Coleridge's confusion did not, however, prevent him from artfully presenting a man who was subject to uncontrolled fits of fear and terror and who, because of those emotions, moved through the entire spectrum of feelings from paralyzing fear to joy. The mariner's final condition of wandering is determined neither by the single emotion of fear nor that of joy, but by the unpredictable and rapid changes in his emotional state and the accompanying alternation between convictions of guilt and hope for salvation. The absolute terror that seizes him in the opening sections is mitigated temporarily by the blessing of the snakes. After a short-lived joy, the agony returns with the unpredictability of a trauma, which, as Lamb so aptly puts it, buries all individuality.

The mariner's eternal punishment is that he must relive his voyage from beginning to end. It was, initially, a mental journey, and, in the telling, the tale is also a mental journey experienced with the

[38] Christopher Wordsworth, *Memoirs*, I, 107.

same intensity as the first. His "strange power of speech" was first acquired at a "dear ransom" of his life's blood and enabled him to retell and thus to be continuously aware of his fears. His prophetic voice is attained at the price of having acquired an irrational and uncontrolled force that compels him to speak.

The mariner's prophetic voice transfixes the wedding guest, so that the mariner's experiences become his listener's. At first the guest is indignant at being interrupted on his walk to the church and is impatient to be released so that he can witness the sacrament of marriage. He thinks the mariner a lunatic and insults him by calling him a "grey-beard loon." But his power of resistence is immediately broken:

> He holds him with his glittering eye—
> The Wedding-Guest stood still,
> And listens like a three years' child:
> The Mariner hath his will.
>
> [ll. 13–16]

The mariner has "his will" in the sense that he is permitted to tell his story, but also in the sense that he has captured the will of the wedding guest. Unaware of what he will hear, the wedding guest listens in wonder and astonishment and remains entranced until the moment when the mariner relates the killing of the albatross. Roused to sympathy by the mariner's story of his persecution, the wedding guest says, "God save thee . . ."

The wedding guest is stunned into silence by the history of the voyage after the killing of the bird until he is told of the death of the crew members. Awe and astonishment give way gradually to the single emotion of fear at the beginning of Part IV when the wedding guest again interrupts the narrative:

> "I fear thee, ancient Mariner!
> I fear thy skinny hand!
> And thou art long, and lank, and brown,
> As is the ribbed sea-sand.
>
> I fear thee and thy glittering eye,
> And thy skinny hand, so brown."
>
> [ll. 224–29]

The wedding guest believes that the mariner has returned from the dead and tries to account for the mariner's appearance the best way he can. The mariner assures him that he was not one of those who died; yet this does not diminish the wedding guest's fear. He again repeats "I fear thee, ancient Mariner" (l. 345) after the blessing of the watersnakes and the arrival of the storm.

Finally the mariner leaves the wedding guest with the moral of his tale. The wedding guest

> Turned from the bridegroom's door.
>
> He went like one that hath been stunned,
> And is of sense forlorn:
> A sadder and a wiser man,
> He rose the morrow morn.
>
> [ll. 621–25]

The wedding guest's being "of sense forlorn" means more than that he has been stunned. "Sense" refers both to sensation and comprehension. "Forlorn" adds to the serious implications, for the word strongly implies that the wedding guest is as affected by the tale as the mariner himself and that his loss of sensation and comprehension equals the mariner's. The mariner's experiences are duplicated in the wedding guest. There is a terrible irony in the mariner's tell-the wedding guest

> O sweeter than the marriage-feast,
> 'Tis sweeter far to me,
> To walk together to the kirk
> With a goodly company!—
>
> [ll. 601–4]

He has prevented the wedding guest from both walking to the church with his company and attending a marriage ceremony. Thus the wedding guest, like the mariner, is removed from the blessings that the mariner says are the greatest pleasures.

The wedding guest is a psychological double of the mariner. The mariner conquers him just as the nightmare conquers the mariner. The wedding guest listens at first with innocence and wonder, but quickly realizes the horror. He is paralyzed by fear, just as the mariner is, and is transfixed by the mariner's gaze, just as the mariner is frozen in "loneliness and fixedness." What little we know of his reaction to the story indicates that his was a constant fear unabated by moments of happiness. Thus the mariner's supplanting the hermit as a spiritual guide and his preventing the guest's attendance at the wedding give the mariner a posthumous, rather than prophetic, voice.

Chapter V

Remorse: *The Poison-Tree*

The nightmare of "The Ancient Mariner" was not a temporary change from a more typical literature of joy and visionary delight. During the months at Nether Stowey in company with Wordsworth, Coleridge often thought and wrote about the problem of evil. While he wrote some superb Conversation Poems in which he reached out toward a community of minds, he spent more time and energy exploring his own mind and the conditions of isolation and loss in which those poems began. "The Wanderings of Cain" and "The Three Graves," both curse poems, as well as *Osorio,* "The Ancient Mariner," and the first part of "Christabel" were all composed within a year, from the summer of 1797 to late spring of 1798. Wordsworth's two major works prior to the summer of 1797, *The Borderers* and "Salisbury Plain," concerned the same issues.

The immediate occasion for *Osorio* was the request from Richard Brinsley Sheridan, forwarded through William Bowles, that Coleridge write a tragedy. He began work in March 1797 and by May had written fifteen hundred lines. About the middle of September he went to visit Bowles for a week with a rough draft of the tragedy. Bowles and William Linley, Sheridan's brother-in-law, suggested some revisions, and in October he sent a revised copy to Bowles, who was asked to forward it to Sheridan. Coleridge told Bowles that he had particular problems with the minor characters, and, probably with a sigh of relief that the work was sent off, also informed Bowles that he had "fagged so long at the work" and saw "so many imperfections in the original & main plot, that I feel an indescribable disgust, a sickness of the very heart, at the mention of the Tragedy" (*CL,* I, 356). By early December he had received the anticipated reply concerning its fitness for the stage: "Sheridan rejects the Tragedy—his *sole* objection is—the obscurity of the three last acts" (*CL,* I, 358). In the following months during negotiations with Cottle over the publication of his and Wordsworth's poems, he thought of publishing *Osorio,* but in the hurry of getting out *Lyrical Ballads* and preparing for the trip to Germany in the fall, the project seems to have been put aside.

Sheridan's complaints about the obscurity of the last three acts must have had the same deadening influence upon Coleridge as did similar criticisms of "The Ancient Mariner." He acknowledged, in a manuscript Preface copied by Clement Carlyon in Germany, that "all is imperfect, and much obscure. Among other equally great defects (millstones round the slender neck of its merits) it presupposes a long story; and this long story, which yet is necessary to the complete understanding of the play, is not half told." From the project he learned "a most important lesson, namely, that to have conceived strongly, does not always imply the power of successful execution" (*PW,* II, 1114). Yet while he reluctantly admitted the play's deficiencies, he was eager to defend it "as a *metaphysician*" (*CL,* I, 604), and maintained that, although the "growth of Osorio's character is nowhere explained," he "had most clear and psychologically accurate ideas of the whole of it . . . A man, who from the constitutional calmness of appetites, is seduced into pride and the love of power, by these into misanthropism, or rather a contempt of mankind, and from thence, by the co-operation of envy, and a curiously modified love for a beautiful female (which is nowhere developed in the play), into a most atrocious guilt. A man who is in truth a weak man, yet always duping himself into the belief that he has a soul of iron" (*PW,* II, 1114). This may have been, in Coleridge's mind, the character he introduced, but it is not a description of what happens to that character during the play.

The manuscript from which Carlyon copied the Preface was with Coleridge in Germany and at Greta Hall while he was living in the Lake District in 1801.[1] He planned to revise and publish it as a poem, but the project languished until 1807, when a number of major revisions were made. The title was changed to *Remorse,* and many of the names were altered. *Remorse* begins with a scene that is not in *Osorio*. Alvar and his companion, Zulimez, have just returned to the Spanish coast and are planning revenge against Alvar's brother, Ordonio, who had conspired to have Alvar murdered:

> *Alvar.* The more behoves it I should rouse within him
> Remorse! that I should save him from himself.
> *Zulimez.* Remorse is as the heart in which it grows:
> If that be gentle, it drops balmy dews
> Of true repentance; but if proud and gloomy,
> It is a poison-tree, that pierced to the inmost
> Weeps only tears of poison!
>
> [I.i.18–24]

[1] A history of the manuscripts and Coleridge's revisions is presented in Paul Zall, "Coleridge's Unpublished Revisions to 'Osorio,'" *BNYPL,* 71 (1967), 516–23.

Coleridge used Zulimez's words as the motto for the play. The ambiguous function of remorse and conscience is explained again by Alvar in the very last lines:

> In these strange dread events
> Just Heaven instructs us with an awful voice,
> That Conscience rules us e'en against our choice.
> Our inward Monitress to guide or warn,
> If listened to; but if repelled with scorn,
> At length as dire Remorse, she reappears,
> Works in our guilty hopes, and selfish fears!
> Still bids, Remember! and still cries, Too Late!
> And while she scares us, goads us to our fate.
>
> [V.i.286–94]

Alvar learns in the progress of the play what Coleridge explained to Southey after the play was produced: "By REMORSE I mean Anguish & Disquietude arising from the Self-contradiction introduced into the Soul by Guilt—a feeling, which is good or bad according as the Will makes use of it. This is exprest in the lines chosen as the Motto—& Remorse is every where distinguished from virtuous Penitence" (*CL,* III, 433–34).

If much of the earlier *Osorio* appeared confused, there is later no confusion about the psychological progress of Ordonio's decline into the nightmare, the denial of his own self, and his suicide by submission to Alhadra's revenge. Ordonio is so weakened that his suicide requires no overt act. His debility is suggested in the first scenes when he is reminded of his deeds and increases as he is forced again and again to recollect his past affection for his brother. Like the mariner, he retreats from reality, and the external reality fades from his sight when the nightmare reality becomes vivid. Sheridan's "*sole* objection" was the result of his misunderstanding Coleridge's metaphysics of guilt; Coleridge had just grounds for claiming that he had conceived of the character firmly.

The nightmare reality first visits Ordonio when he asks Isidore to play the role of a sorcerer and to convince Teresa that Alvar is dead. Isidore surprises Ordonio when he tells him that during the attempted assassination, the two conspirators who attacked Alvar were wounded and forced to confess that they had been hired by Ordonio, and that the murder would remove a barrier between Ordonio and the woman who loved him. Ordonio's reaction to hearing that Alvar surrendered himself to the assassination is a further step into the nightmares of his conscience:

> *Ordonio.* And you kill'd him?
> Oh blood hounds! may eternal wrath flame round you!
> He was his Maker's Image undefac'd!
> It seizes me—by Hell I will go on!
> What—would'st thou stop, man? thy pale looks won't save thee!
> Oh cold—cold—cold! shot through with icy cold!
>
> [II.i.118–23]

Ordonio's imagination has created a picture of the assassination in which Alvar is a god pursued by the hounds of hell. The impression is so vivid that Ordonio actually sees the assassination, which he does not know did not occur, well before Alvar, dressed as the sorcerer, places the painting of it before him. Like the mariner who returns time and time again to the image of the albatross, Ordonio sinks into a nightmare dominated by the one image representative of his guilt.

Alvar had asked Isidore to deliver to Ordonio the message that the disguised Alvar was one who "can bring the dead to life again" (II.ii.71). Alvar is a painter, an artist who can fix one moment of the past upon canvas and make it appear to be a substantial reality to Ordonio, who, unknown to Alvar, has just thought of that very scene. In the earlier *Osorio,* Ordonio (Osorio) does not see the painting of the assassination because he is in a stupor from Alvar's (Albert's) accusations. After writing the first draft, Coleridge learned that the seeing of the fixed image and the stupor of guilt were the same thing. Thus in *Remorse* Ordonio views the painting. He remains in a stupor amid the confusion of the incense-filled room, the arrival of Monviedro, and the scuffle of Alvar's arrest.

Ordonio recomposes himself during the scuffle and later explains to Valdez, his father, that he had planned the scene to expose the sorcerer to the scrutiny of the Inquisition. Valdez, sensing perhaps that Ordonio's explanations are not sufficient, asks him whether he knows what the speeches of the sorcerer meant:

> *Valdez.* But have you yet discovered
> (Where is Teresa?) what those speeches meant—
> Pride, and hypocrisy, and guilt, and cunning?
> Then when the wizard fix'd his eye on you,
> And you, I know not why, look'd pale and trembled—
> Why—why, what ails you now?—
>
> [III.ii.62–67]

Valdez unknowingly repeats Alvar's accusations, and again Ordonio is thrown into a fit by the recollection in which he vacillates between trying to laugh off his former distraction, by calling a pricking of his conscience a "pricking of the blood," and returning to his stupor by repeating the line that he had uttered in it, "Dup'd! Dup'd! Dup'd!" The feeling of betrayal is not merely a convenient device to keep the plot going. The conviction that he has been betrayed also stabs deeper than if it were merely the insubordinate act of an unfaithful conspirator, because it was an ingredient of nightmares.

Teresa, who has become suspicious of Ordonio, steps in front of him with the intention of questioning him. Sensing that he is being again challenged, he asks, "Teresa? or the phantom of Teresa?" Her demand to know where Alvar's corpse is buried is answered by another of Ordonio's fits. While he points to the "sleep-compelling earth," he says, "For while we live— / An inward day that never, never sets, / Glares round the soul, and mocks the closing eyelids" (III.ii.123–26). He wishes for a death, a death which is realized in the final act.

If Alvar intended to lead Ordonio to repentance, he diagnosed Ordonio's ills badly. He induces in Ordonio a nightmare, which is reinforced by Valdez and Teresa, both of whom suspect that something is wrong, and which creates a greater evil making repentance impossible. Ordonio resolves immediately to kill Isidore, to strike out against that which betrays him; Alvar's ministrations bring more crimes. The fourth act begins with Isidore alone in the cavern where Ordonio meets him. Isidore has had premonitions of disaster and sees in a pit in the cave "the very same I dreamt of!" (IV.i.13). When Ordonio emerges from the darkness, Isidore says that he had almost stepped into the pit. Fear pulls him back from the edge, and he tells Ordonio of his previous night's dream:

> O sleep of horrors! Now run down and stared at
> By forms so hideous that they mock remembrance—
> Now seeing nothing and imagining nothing,
> But only being afraid—stifled with fear!
> While every goodly or familiar form
> Had a strange power of breathing terror round me!
>
> [IV.i.68–73]

In May 1814 Coleridge himself quoted these six lines, with minor variations, when he described his addiction to opium, and called the lines "Another Fragment on the Night Mair" (*CL,* III, 496). He also printed a variant in the *Biographia* to explain Wordsworth's genius, "a state, which spreads its influence and coloring over all, that co-exists with the exciting cause, and in which

> 'The Simplest, and the most familiar things
> Gain a strange power of spreading awe around them. . . .'"
>
> [*BL,* II, 54–55]

By printing the lines as they originally stood in *Remorse* as a footnote in the *Biographia,* Coleridge invited a comparison of the nightmare he experienced with the quite different power of Wordsworth's imagination.

A manuscript note to *Osorio* justifies the inclusion in the play of what Coleridge called "prophetical dreams" as more than mere superstitions:

> This will be held by many for a mere Tragedy-dream—by many who have never given themselves the trouble to ask themselves from what grounds dreams pleased in Tragedy, and wherefore they have been so common. I believe, however, that in the present case, the whole is psychologically true and accurate. Prophetical dreams are things of nature, and explicable by that law of the mind in which where dim ideas are connected with vivid feelings, Perception and Imagination insinuate themselves and mix with the forms of Recollection, till the Present appears to exactly correspond with the Past. Whatever is partially like, the Imagination will gradually represent as wholly like—a law of our nature which, when it is perfectly understood, woe to the great city Babylon—to all the superstitions of Men!
>
> [*PW,* II, 565–66]

Isidore sees "it now more clearly, / Than in my dream I saw—that very chasm" (IV.i.80–81). His nightmare, which complements Ordonio's, becomes real. Isidore knows that he did not kill Alvar but assumes that since Alvar has not returned, he is dead, and that he contributed to Alvar's death by telling Alvar that Teresa did not love him. Isidore feels guilty for killing Alvar's hope; Isidore's fear transforms the entire scene into a dreadful dream of vengeance. When Ordonio thrusts Isidore down into the pit, he mocks Isidore: "His dream too is made out" (IV.i.171). Of course Ordonio does not yet understand the irony in his words. He has just finished telling Isidore of his version of his fall into crime, one which he says was caused by his giving a reality to the shadows of his imagination. His explanation of the desire to murder Alvar actually describes his nightmare; his dream, too, will be made out.

From the cavern where he has murdered Isidore, Ordonio rushes to the dungeon in which Alvar, still disguised as the sorcerer, is imprisoned. If the cavern represents the imagination in its darkest moods and most depraved manifestations, the dungeon represents the misery that man inflicts upon man. The political themes are more explicit than the psychological ones in Alvar's soliloquy at the beginning of the last act:

> Each pore and natural outlet shrivelled up
> By ignorance and parching poverty,
> His energies roll back upon his heart,
> And stagnate and corrupt, till, chang'd to poison,

> They break out on him, like a loathsome plague-spot!
> Then we call in our pampered mountebanks:
> And this is their best cure! uncomforted
> And friendless solitude, groaning and tears,
> And savage faces, at the clanking hour,
> Seen through the steam and vapours of his dungeon
> By the lamp's dismal twilight! So he lies
> Circled with evil, till his very soul
> Unmoulds its essence, hopelessly deformed
> By sights of evermore deformity!
>
> [V.i.6–19]

Yet the political evil in unjust and inhumane imprisonment is stated in psychological terms. The inhumanity of arbitrary imprisonment is the mental isolation. The mind is forced into itself, and its vital energies stagnate into poisons. Alvar is pushed toward the nightmare by being imprisoned, but this soliloquy is the closest he comes to understanding it until after Ordonio's death.

Ordonio is possessed by the idea that he must destroy Alvar, who, he believes, conspired with Isidore to expose his guilt. Alvar tells Ordonio that his boasting is the "revelry of a drunken anguish, / Which fain would scoff away the pang of guilt" (V.i.119–20). Ordonio answers Alvar's insistence that he could be saved with an uncomprehending repetition of "Saved? Saved?" (V.i.166). Obsessed with the recent murder of Isidore and the compulsion to murder again, Ordonio cannot be moved by Alvar's shallow piety. Isidore's murder, of which Alvar has no knowledge, is foremost in Ordonio's mind when Alvar tries to lead him to remorse:

> *Ordonio.* He told me of the babes that prattled to him,
> His fatherless little ones! remorse! remorse!
> Where got'st thou that fool's word? Curse on remorse!
> Can it give up the dead, or recompact
> A mangled body? mangled—dashed to atoms!
> Not all the blessings of a host of angels
> Can blow away a desolate widow's curse!
> And though thou spill thy heart's blood for atonement,
> It will not weigh against an orphan's tear!
>
> [V.i.168–76]

Alvar has no idea of what Ordonio is talking about, repeats his own name, and hopes that Ordonio will return to a distinct recollection of the attempted fratricide, but Ordonio dwells on Isidore's murder. Alvar tries again to recall the fratricide. This time Ordonio responds but sees Alvar as a phantom. Alvar removes his disguise and reveals that he is not a sorcerer, whereupon Ordonio kneels before him and asks to be cursed with forgiveness.

As Alvar calls for repentance, Teresa notices that Ordonio's eyes are staring blankly into space. The real scene in front of him has vanished, and he sees again the murdered Isidore coming toward him. Thus as Alvar is transformed in Ordonio's mind from a ghost into a living person, he fades from Ordonio's mind because to Ordonio only the haunting phantoms are real. Alvar's image is replaced by Isidore's:

> *Ordonio.* Nearer and nearer! and I can not stir!
> Will no one hear these stifled groans, and wake me?
> He would have died to save me, and I killed him—
> A husband and a father!—
>
> [V.i.221–24]

These lines are in the original *Osorio,* and in March 1806 Coleridge used one of them in a notebook entry:

> I know tis but a Dream, yet feel more anguish
> Than if 'twere Truth. It has been often so,
> Must I die under it? Is no one near?
> Will no one hear these stifled groans, & wake me?
>
> [*NB,* II, 2799]

It is probable that Coleridge was working on revisions of *Osorio* at the time this note was written. By applying Ordonio's line to himself, he makes the same kind of identification of himself with Ordonio as he did of himself with the mariner. Coburn's identification of Osorio with Southey may be appropriate for the first drafts of the play, but Coleridge later saw much of himself in Ordonio (*NB,* II, 2928n).

In the midst of Ordonio's distraction, Alhadra and the Moors break into the dungeon, seeking Ordonio and revenge. Ordonio immediately finds that the dream corresponds to the reality. Alvar and Teresa are transfixed with horror at his admission of murder. Teresa recovers enough to think that Ordonio repents, but she is clearly wrong. While Alhadra curses Ordonio, cries are heard from Valdez and his men, so Alhadra stabs Ordonio, who, as he dies, says:

> She hath avenged the blood of Isidore!
> I stood in silence like a slave before her
> That I might taste the wormwood and the gall,
> And satiate this self-accusing heart
> With bitterer agonies than death can give.
>
> [V.i.259–63]

Like Isidore's, his dream is made out. Alvar has learned that his plan has failed and that remorse destroys someone whose conscience turns to poison. His final words are an admission that he does not take Ordonio's dying cry of "Atonement" to be a final salvation.[2]

Coleridge's tragedy was, as he said, "certainly a great favourite of mine, the more so, as certain pet abstract notions of mine are therein expounded."[3] The "pet abstract notions" to which he refers must be those with which he could have defended *Osorio* to Sheridan and Linley and similar to those he embodied in "The Ancient Mariner." They deal with the psychology of guilt, ideas that were familiar to him by the time of the first production of *Remorse* in 1813. Coleridge told Southey, "As from a circumference to a centre, every Ray in the Tragedy converges to Ordonio" (*CL,* III, 434).

[2] Ordonio's cry of "Atonement" was not in the first printed version of *Remorse.*
[3] Allsop, p. 65.

Chapter VI

"Christabel": A Ghost by Day Time

Coleridge invited a comparison of "Christabel" with "Kubla Khan" by publishing them with "The Pains of Sleep" in one volume in 1816. He recognized in "Kubla Khan" that the energy necessary for poetry can not always be given a permanent form and that within the imaginative dream are forces that destroy it. The dream of "Kubla Khan" was rendered insubstantial and unreal. Images that were once clearly held in the mind faded until they finally dissolved. After "Kubla Khan" there is the added fear that what is represented in the dream may become a vivid reality of horror rather than a mere airy nothing, a flitting phantasy. There is, also, a reversal of Coleridge's expectations for the symbol apprehended in a dream. If once he expected the symbol to shadow forth spiritual truths and to reconcile objective reality and the subjective experience, he later found that, isolated from externality, the symbol became a stark reflection of the reality within. "Christabel," like so many of Coleridge's other poems, begins with a dream or an imaginative conception that in earlier poems he tried to verify by sensation or by the experience of other minds, but Christabel's dream is proved to be in no sense a liberation. The poem opens in her night's dream; the second section opens at dawn, when Geraldine, previously a creature of the dream and dependent for her existence upon Christabel, becomes real in the daylight. The poetry that Coleridge hoped would be a waking dream becomes even more explicitly a waking nightmare.

Christabel sets out from the castle to pray for her lover, but instead she is conquered by her dream. Geraldine, who is found pale and weak in the forest of Christabel's dream, first appears as an insubstantial specter. Geraldine begs for assistance and is ushered into the castle, where Christabel innocently carries her over the threshold and invites her to share her bed. Within the walls of the castle Geraldine gains a strange power over Christabel, until Geraldine is no longer a mere phantom conceived in Christabel's mind but has become a reality apart from the dream and embodies instincts that Christabel cannot control. Geraldine becomes more and more active as she gains ascendancy over Christabel, while Christabel, who had previously been active, is reduced to passivity. Geraldine's gradual transformation in Christabel's sight, from a strange and beautiful woman to a hideous hag parallels Christabel's awareness of the evil that she herself has produced.

The poem ends with Christabel completely paralyzed by Geraldine's spell. Coleridge was as responsible as anyone for the rumors that he had the entire plan of five cantos in his mind before he began. He wrote to Byron in 1815, "I should say, that the plan of the whole poem was formed and the first Book and half of the second were finished—and it was not till after my return from Germany in the year 1800 that I resumed it—and finished the second and a part of the third Book" (*CL,* IV, 601). There are also the statements made during the composition of the second part in preparation for the second edition of *Lyrical Ballads* that the poem had reached thirteen or fourteen hundred lines, more than twice the length of the texts printed (*CL,* I, 631,634). Perhaps Thomas Allsop's record of Coleridge's conversation is nearer the truth: "I had the whole of the two cantos in my mind before I began it; certainly, the first canto is more perfect, has more of the true wild weird spirit, than the last."[1] Mr. Justice Coleridge was once told by Wordsworth that Coleridge "had no idea how 'Christabelle' was to have been finished, and he did not think my uncle had ever conceived, in his own mind, any definite plan for it."[2] With Coleridge working intensely to finish it for *Lyrical Ballads* and in daily communication with him, Wordsworth would certainly have known whether Coleridge had planned the entire five cantos.

Another statement recorded by Allsop puts into perspective the prose summary of the final sections that Gillman offered: "If I should finish 'Christabel,' I shall certainly extend it, and give new characters, and a greater number of incidents. This the 'reading public' require, and this is the reason that Sir Walter Scott's poems, though so loosely written, are pleasing, and interest us by their picturesqueness."[3] Gillman had written that Coleridge planned to have Bracy set out on his mission to inform Geraldine's father that she is safe with the baron, but Geraldine, knowing that she can no longer impersonate Lord Roland's daughter, disappears. She reappears as Christabel's lover, who is still absent, and courts Christabel, who does not return the affection. Christabel's father takes her reserve as a personal affront to himself and to the knight and insists that she marry him. She acquiesces, but at the wedding ceremony the real

[1] Allsop, p. 64.

[2] Grosart, III, 427. Wordsworth told Alexander Dyce that Coleridge "certainly wrote no more of *Christabel* than has appeared in print" (Dyce, p. 185).

[3] Allsop, p. 64.

knight and lover arrives with the ring that Christabel had given him. Geraldine is thus exposed and vanishes, after which Christabel marries the knight, and father and daughter are reconciled.[4]

This summary is probably a fabrication produced for Gillman years after Coleridge finished the second part. The difficulty in accepting such a plot continuance is that it does not grow naturally out of the sections already written. Christabel has been rendered utterly passive, and in Gillman's account she is saved only by the return of her former lover, who produces the ring. She is saved by an intercession when the restoration must come from within; for any conclusion to be convincing she must cope with her own evil. Furthermore, Gillman's account does not support the moral that he himself gives:

> The story of the Christabel is partly founded on the notion, that the virtuous of this world save the wicked. The pious and good Christabel suffers and prays for
>
> "The weal of her lover that is far away,"
>
> exposed to various temptations in a foreign land; and she thus defeats the power of evil represented in the person of Geraldine. This is one main object of the tale.[5]

In Gillman's summary, Christabel's passive suffering has little effect upon the knight's exploits and spiritual state. Coleridge misled his friends into thinking that the narrative was incomplete when the psychology of Christabel's discovery of evil was complete.

Like so many misconceptions fostered about Coleridge's intentions, the "main object of the tale" offered by Gillman may originally have come from Coleridge himself. He told Allsop in 1821 that when he wrote the poem, Crashaw's lines on Saint Theresa "were ever present to my mind while writing the second part of Christabel; if, indeed, by some subtle process of the mind, they did not suggest the first thought of the whole poem":

> Since 'tis not to be had at home,
> She'll travel to a martyrdome.
> No home for her confesses she,
> But where she may a martyr be.
> She'll to the Moores, and trade with them
> For this invalued diadem,
> She offers them her dearest breath
> With Christ's name in't, in change for death.

[4] Gillman, pp. 301–2.
[5] *Ibid.*, p. 283.

She'll bargain with them, and will give
Them God, and teach them how to live
In Him, or if they this deny,
For Him she'll teach them how to die.
So shall she leave among them sown,
The Lord's blood, or, at least her own.
Farewell then, all the world—adieu,
Teresa is no more for you:
Farewell all pleasures, sports, and joys,
Never till now esteemed toys—
Farewell whatever dear'st may be,
Mother's arm or father's knee;
Farewell house, and farewell home,
She's for the Moores and martyrdom.[6]

Coleridge's reference to Crashaw implies that Christabel suffers for her lover and wins martyrdom, but we cannot be sure that Coleridge's reference to Saint Theresa is exclusively to these lines. Perhaps Coleridge was recalling the biography he had read. He jotted down a long note in *The Works of the Holy Mother St. Teresa* that formed the basis of his discussion of her in the *Philosophical Lectures* several years later, when he spoke of her as one "of that class of beings who would have religion without any mixture of intellect." Her imagination nurtured by romances, accustomed to a mystic Spanish Catholicism and intensely emotional, she was inflamed with an ecstatic love of God, and at an early age decided to join a nunnery. Her superstitious father, Coleridge added, was wise enough "to perceive how utterly unfit such a nursery of inward fancies and outward privations was to a brain, heart, and bodily constitution, like that of innocent, loving and high-impassioned Teresa. What could come of it but a despairing anguish-stricken sinner, or a mad saint?" Suppression of her natural instincts in the nunnery led to a host of physical ailments and fainting fits. Her desire for martyrdom and love of God combined with her lack of intellect to make it impossible

that a woman so innocent and so susceptible, of an imagination so lively by nature, and so fever-kindled by disease and its occasions, (and this so well furnished with the requisite images and pre-conceptions), should not mistake, and often, the less painful and in such a form the sometimes pleasurable approaches to bodily deliquium, and her imperfect fainting-fits, for divine transports and momentary union with God. Especially if, with a thoughtful yet pure psychology, you join the force of suppressed instincts stirring in the heart and bodily frame, of a mind unconscious of their nature, and these in

[6] Allsop, pp. 117–18. Allsop quotes Crashaw's "A Hymn to the Name and Honor of the Admirable Saint Teresa."

the keenly sensitive body, in the innocent and loving soul of Teresa, with "all her thirsts, and lives, and deaths of love" and what remains unsolved, for which the credulity of the many and the knavery of a few will not furnish ample explanation?[7]

The insight is typically Coleridgean. A lively imagination, an often diseased body, and suppressed and unconscious instincts are the conditions under which the mind surrenders to its own fancies and cannot understand that sanity depends upon a clear conception of the reality that is within and the reality without. If Coleridge's initial reference to Saint Theresa is to his analysis in the lectures and not exclusively to the lines that Allsop prints from Crashaw, then the reference to Saint Theresa coincides with the picture of Christabel in the poem while it accounts for Gillman's misunderstanding.

Christabel is a Saint Theresa who, in her dreams, leaves the shelter of her father's castle and travels to the oak covered with moss and mistletoe, suggestive of pagan worship, where she prays for her lover:

She had dreams all yesternight
Of her own betrothéd knight;
And she in the midnight wood will pray
For the weal of her lover that's far away.

[ll. 27–30]

Her travels are, like those of Saint Theresa, in her imagination, and, like those of the ancient mariner, in a world in which the ordinary referents of time and space are dislocated. The cock, the harbinger of dawn, is awakened at midnight by the cries of the owls. The sounds of night have wakened the dawn, a theme that is continuously kept in mind in the second part when the horrors of night become the evil of the day.

The setting of the April midnight is ominous. The ancient mastiff sees a shroud, and the sky is covered with thin clouds that make the moon appear "both small and dull," an anticipation of the glance Geraldine gives to Christabel in Part II with a snake's "small eye" that is "dull and shy" (l. 583). Praying under the old oak, Christabel hears a moaning from the other side and looks to see the cause:

There she sees a damsel bright,
Drest in a silken robe of white,
That shadowy in the moonlight shone:
The neck that made that white robe wan,
Her stately neck, and arms were bare;
Her blue-veined feet unsandal'd were,

[7] *PL,* pp. 313–16. Coleridge quotes from Crashaw's "The Flaming Heart." The original note is printed in *LR,* IV, 68–71.

And wildly glittered here and there
The gems entangled in her hair.

[ll. 58–65]

Christabel's fright resembles that of the mariner upon seeing the Night-mare Life-in-Death, whose skin is as white as leprosy. Her first question parallels that of the hermit, who asks the mariner, "What manner of man art thou?" Christabel asks, "And who art thou?" Both the hermit and Christabel fear that the person they see has come from the dead. In response, Geraldine provides an answer that, for the moment, convinces Christabel that she has been abducted by five horsemen, who transported her across "the shade of night" (l. 87).

Before and after she tells her story, Geraldine begs Christabel to stretch forth her hand and assist her to flee from her captors who, she said, promised to return shortly. Assured that she has nothing to fear, Christabel assents to her request and reaches out, promising hospitality and protection in her father's hall. Again Christabel must touch Geraldine when they cross the threshold into the castle, and finally when they lie down to sleep Geraldine says:

"In the touch of this bosom there worketh a spell,
Which is lord of thy utterance, Christabel!
Thou knowest to-night, and wilt know to-morrow,
This mark of my shame, this seal of my sorrow. . . ."

[ll. 267–70]

Christabel's carrying Geraldine over the threshold is an example of the common folk theme that evil beings cannot enter a sanctified place unaided. But since only a few of the instances of touch can be explained by traditional lore about supernatural beings, it is all too easy to assume that Coleridge is writing about perverse sexuality. He is more consciously picturing the means by which one is assured that what one sees is real. By touching Geraldine, Christabel is assured that she is real, for to Christabel she appears as a phantom. Coleridge knew that sight often deceives, and, like Berkeley before him, was willing to believe that touch verifies sight. Thus the repeated motif of touch, whatever it may imply of perverse sexuality, demonstrates the way in which a dream becomes actuality.

The foreboding that Geraldine will prove to be an evil influence increases as she is assisted toward Christabel's chamber. The mastiff moans, the torch flares in the hall, and, once within the chamber, Geraldine faints when Christabel trims the lamp that illuminates the carved angels. Christabel offers Geraldine a restorative wine her mother has made. Geraldine asks whether Christabel's mother will pity her, and Christabel replies that she will, exclaiming, "O mother dear! that thou were here!" (l. 202). Geraldine immediately echoes her: "I would, said Geraldine, she were!" This is the only time that Geraldine echoes Christabel; later their roles are reversed when Christabel passively imitates Geraldine.

A momentary traumatic fit grips Geraldine. Her voice changes, and she tries to assume the powers of Christabel's guardian spirit, her mother:

> "Off, wandering mother! Peak and pine!
> I have power to bid thee flee."
> Alas! what ails poor Geraldine?
> Why stares she with unsettled eye?
> Can she the bodiless dead espy?
> And why with hollow voice cries she,
> "Off, woman, off! this hour is mine—
> Though thou her guardian spirit be,
> Off, woman, off! 'tis given to me."
>
> [ll. 205–13]

The phrase "peak and pine" is spoken by the First Witch in *Macbeth:* "Weary se'nnights nine times nine / Shall he dwindle, peak and pine" (I.iii.22–23). Of the Weird Sisters Coleridge is reported to have said: "Their character consists in the imaginative disconnected from the good; they are the shadowy obscure and fearfully anomalous of physical nature, the lawless of human nature,—elemental avengers without sex or kin."[8] Derwent Coleridge's denial that Geraldine was a "witch or goblin, or malignant being of any kind"[9] was perhaps an attempt to dissociate Geraldine from the witches in *Macbeth,* an association that might easily be made from the repetition of the phrase "peak and pine." In an obvious sense he is correct; but, on the other hand, Geraldine is "imagination disconnected from the good," a shadow figure whose uncertain sexuality left Coleridge with qualms about the public's reception of the obscure references to improper sexual relations between Geraldine and Christabel. But, more importantly, imagination severed from the good must, as Coleridge too well knew, become an avenger, a force that turns against its creator who can no longer command its powers.

During this night the power is granted to Geraldine for only a

[8] *SC,* I, 67 n. 2. T. M. Raysor considers this to be H. N. Coleridge's interpolation.

[9] Both A. H. Nethercot (*The Road to Tryermaine* [Chicago: Univ. of Chicago Press, 1939], p. 41 n. 3) and House (p. 127 n. 1) admit to being unable to find the original of this statement and use as their authority E. H. Coleridge's edition of *Christabel* (London: Frowde, 1907), p. 52. E. H. C. refers to an undated edition of Derwent and Sara Coleridge's *The Poems of Samuel Taylor Coleridge* (London: Moxon, 1870?), p. xlii.

moment:

> Then Christabel knelt by the lady's side,
> And raised to heaven her eyes so blue—
> Alas! said she, this ghastly ride—
> Dear lady! it hath wildered you!
> The lady wiped her moist cold brow,
> And faintly said, " 'tis over now!"
>
> [ll. 214–19]

She is more possessed than possessing, lending credence to Derwent Coleridge's interpretation that she is not a witch or "malignant being of any kind, but a spirit, executing her appointed task with the best good will." There is the possibility, were the poem completed successfully along the lines that Coleridge later described, that Geraldine is sent, against her will, to tempt Christabel and to be the evil that must be defeated, as the good suffer for others and bring about their redemption. Geraldine's momentary fit is over, and she sympathetically assures Christabel of her protection:

> All they who live in the upper sky,
> Do love you, holy Christabel!
> And you love them, and for their sake
> And for the good which me befel,
> Even I in my degree will try,
> Fair maiden, to requite you well.
>
> [ll. 227–32]

Perhaps satisfied that she has rescued a woman from evil and yet unaware of the evil she has conducted into the sanctuary of the castle, Christabel lies down to sleep. Her mind, though, is not tranquil; she has just seen Geraldine pass through a traumatic moment that remains mysterious to her. She cannot free herself from the mystery: "through her brain of weal and woe / So many thoughts moved to and fro, / That vain it were her lids to close" (ll. 239–41). She has become aware of her own confused thoughts as reflected in her inability to organize her impressions. While she lies in bed unable to sleep, she carefully watches Geraldine, unaware that she is seeing, in her disturbed state, her own self. As Geraldine disrobes, Christabel sees the mark of her sin, a mark which Coleridge in the printed text tells us is a "sight to dream of, not to tell" (l. 253), but which in an earlier text he had described as "lean and old and foul of hue."

Just as the roles of the mariner and the hermit are reversed, the roles of Christabel and Geraldine are reversed. The restorative spirituality Christabel offers Geraldine is answered by Geraldine's impressing her mark upon Christabel. The Conclusion to Part I discloses the traumatic fit of a diseased imagination that Geraldine has transferred to Christabel:

> With open eyes (ah woe is me!)
> Asleep, and dreaming fearfully,
> Fearfully dreaming, yet, I wis,
> Dreaming that alone, which is—
> O sorrow and shame!
>
> [ll. 292–96]

Christabel's sleep imprisons her in a nightmare of sorrow and shame. To dream with her eyes open is to mix, as the narrator informs us, the images of the dream with "that alone, which is," the now undeniable fact of Geraldine's presence. Evil, formerly hidden, is now exposed. Shame itself is the fear of exposure, but not yet guilt, a conviction of errancy.

Like Geraldine's brief fit, Christabel's quickly passes:

> And see! the lady Christabel
> Gathers herself from out her trance;
> Her limbs relax, her countenance
> Grows sad and soft; the smooth thin lids
> Close o'er her eyes; and tears she sheds—
> Large tears that leave the lashes bright!
> And oft the while she seems to smile
> As infants at a sudden light!
>
> [ll. 311–18]

Christabel's sleep now becomes a prayer, and she believes her guardian mother is restored to her protective function. As Coleridge was to discover in another context, his meditations on the nature of evil during the winter of 1803–04, evil and innocence are both characteristic of a mind loosened from the restraints of waking thought. Thus both Geraldine and then Christabel go through fits of possession in which both are exposed. Geraldine is a psychological double whom Christabel has constructed unconsciously in her dream, a reflection of herself which at this point in the narrative possesses both good and evil intentions. Geraldine is an unwilling victim of forces that exercise fitful control over her, and she is not yet representative of the pure evil that Christabel sees later. In other words, Geraldine and Christabel are not two halves of one person, the unconscious and the conscious, but mirror images, and Geraldine is the embodiment of the knowledge that Christabel has gained of herself through her wandering. Later Geraldine becomes a double by division, the evil in the unconscious in which Christabel is totally immersed.

The second part of "Christabel," written two years after the first, repeats many of the incidents of the first so that there are close parallels between the two sections. The first part opens with the confusion between night and the dawn; the second, with the coming of dawn that to the baron is the arrival of death. Geraldine is in the first part a dream figure who tells her tale to Christabel; in the second she is a living, substantial woman who tells her tale to the baron, who in turn offers his hospitality and protection, as Christabel did in the first. The dream in the first part is repeated in Bracy's dream in the second. And, most importantly, the fits of possession are repeated, but in the fits, as in the other incidents of the plot, there is an inversion of the first. Where there was recovery from them, there now is none for Christabel.

Geraldine is infused with physical strength, life that has been taken from Christabel much as a vampire sucks life from the living:

And Christabel awoke and spied
The same who lay down by her side—
O rather say, the same whom she
Raised up beneath the old oak tree!
Nay, fairer yet! and yet more fair!
For she belike hath drunken deep
Of all the blessedness of sleep!
And while she spake, her looks, her air
Such gentle thankfulness declare,
That (so it seemed) her girded vests
Grew tight beneath her heaving breasts.

[ll. 370–80]

To Christabel the innocent sleep is at first refreshing, but she shortly discovers that the horror that came upon her the previous night has not left with the coming of day. Watching vivid flashes of lightning in the middle of the day, Coleridge was reminded of the poem: "the terror without the beauty.—A ghost day time / Geraldine" (*NB,* II, 2207). Christabel's response to seeing Geraldine's growth and vitality is "Sure I have sinn'd" (l. 381). Unless one considers that Christabel herself is responsible for Geraldine's continuous life, there is no reason for Christabel's feelings of guilt and her acceptance of personal responsibility, which had been the previous night only intimations of shame. Sleep for Christabel and the mariner is only a temporary respite from the terror. Hers is "such perplexity of mind / As dreams too lively leave behind" (ll. 385–86).

When her father first embraces Geraldine,

a vision fell
Upon the soul of Christabel,
The vision of fear, the touch and pain!

> She shrunk and shuddered, and saw again—
> (Ah, woe is me! Was it for thee,
> Thou gentle maid! such sights to see?)
>
> Again she saw that bosom old,
> Again she felt that bosom cold,
> And drew in her breath with a hissing sound. . . .
>
> [ll. 451–59]

After the baron has heard Geraldine's story, has appointed Bracy to carry the news to Lord Roland de Vaux, and has heard Bracy's dream, Christabel is seized by the vision of evil. The ground is unsteady beneath her when she repeats Geraldine's "hissing sound." Her trance is brought about by her knowledge of her sin and is constituted by the ever-present image of Geraldine, that "sole image in her mind" (l. 604). Christabel is enslaved by that one visual image, so much so that her only possible action is to imitate it. Having created the image herself, she allows it to master her, and under such conditions there is no vital interchange between a creative mind and external reality. The result, all too explicit for Coleridge to hold any hope of altering the situation so that Christabel could save herself, is stagnation. Geraldine has lost whatever positive blessings she possessed the previous night when she prayed that Christabel's guardian spirit would protect her. The one hour that was granted to Geraldine has turned into an eternity.

The second part of "Christabel" is not limited to the effects of evil upon Christabel, however. Poetically there was little to be done with Christabel as a character after she had been reduced to passive imitation of Geraldine; in fact, being so reduced, she ceases to be a person at all. The emphasis falls, in the second part, on the effect Geraldine has upon the baron. Geraldine fights for his allegiance against the baron's love for Christabel and against Bracy, who warns him of Geraldine's evil and Christabel's suffering. This conflict is analogous to the contest in the first part between Geraldine and Christabel's guardian spirit for Christabel's soul. In the second part that conflict is over, and the real interest lies in the resolution of the baron's allegiance. Geraldine is, of course, the victor in each part. The last lines before the Conclusion to Part II describe the baron's turning away from Christabel and leading Geraldine forth. Her victory underlines the pervasive effect of evil once it has been created and the objective reality it can possess; it is no longer a mere figment of Christabel's diseased imagination.

If Christabel is primarily a contemplative person, her father is primarily a man of action. Upon first meeting Geraldine, Christabel fears a supernatural visitation; her father, upon first hearing her story of abduction, reacts with rage. He is a man who trusts the physical world of his senses, and, although religious, and even a bit superstitious, he nevertheless believes that appearances constitute reality. He proclaims that he will challenge the abductors in a tournament in which he boasts that he will sever their "reptile souls" from their bodies. Like the crew in "The Ancient Mariner," he seeks causes and explanations of events in the visible world.

At his proclamation, Geraldine shudders with horror, which the baron mistakes as a sign of aristocratic rage at the injustice done to her, proof that she is the true daughter of Lord Roland de Vaux. Christabel's shudder at her father's embracing Geraldine prompts the baron to inquire what is wrong. Mastered by Geraldine, Christabel can respond only by hoping that "All will yet be well" (l. 472), which is followed by a request to send Geraldine home quickly. The baron, thinking Christabel's request a breach of hospitality and fearing to lose an opportunity of reconciling himself and Lord Roland de Vaux, denies her request and instead orders Bracy to go to Lord Roland's castle to inform him of his daughter's safety and to appoint a time for a ceremonious meeting between the two. Bracy resists the command and justifies his reluctance by relating his dream of the previous night:

> For in my sleep I saw that dove,
> That gentle bird, whom thou dost love,
> And call'st by thy own daughter's name—
> Sir Leoline! I saw the same
> Fluttering, and uttering fearful moan,
> Among the green herbs in the forest alone.
>
> . . . . .
>
> I went and peered, and could descry
> No cause for her distressful cry;
> But yet for her dear lady's sake
> I stooped, methought, the dove to take,
> When lo! I saw a bright green snake
> Coiled around its wings and neck.
>
> [ll. 531–36, 545–50]

When Bracy stoops to free the dove, he awakes, at midnight, the exact hour that Christabel begins her wanderings, and before the dove can be freed. He dreams during Christabel's dream and, repeating the motif of the dream's becoming real, states:

> But though my slumber was gone by,
> This dream it would not pass away—
> It seems to live upon my eye!
>
> [ll. 557–59]

So taken with Geraldine's beauty is the baron that, only half-listening, he misinterprets the dream. His error is not simply a matter of his being obtuse. He is inattentive because he is sure that his initial interpretation that the dove represents Geraldine is true. Christabel falls because she can see nothing but the dream; the baron is deceived because he ignores it.

Christabel is almost struck dumb by her father's interpretation of the dream and by Geraldine's reaction to it. The baron takes her reaction and request that Geraldine be sent away as a violation of the laws of hospitality and an insult to himself. Faced with a moral dilemma, the necessity of either acceding to the wishes of his daughter, for whom his dying wife prayed, or fulfilling his promise of hospitality, he is thrown into confusion: "If thoughts, like these, had any share, / They only swelled his rage and pain, / And did but work confusion there" (ll. 637–39).

The partial shift in focus from Christabel to the baron may be explained by a number of reasons, the most obvious of which is Coleridge's uncertainty about his own role as a father. The Conclusion to Part II indicates clearly that this might be true. It originally was not written as a part of "Christabel," but as a poem about his son Hartley in 1801 and sent to Southey with the affectionate footnote "A very metaphysical account of Fathers calling their children rogues, rascals, & little varlets" (*CL,* II, 729). The Conclusion is not entirely consistent with "Christabel" if the poem is read solely as Christabel's story, because she is responsible for admitting evil into the castle. The Conclusion paints the portrait of unconscious innocence and joy, which is met with an excess of paternal affection, which, because of its excess, turns to harshness and reproach. But if the second part is read as the baron's story, the last lines of the Conclusion summarize the results of Christabel's dream becoming reality and producing evil:

> And what, if in a world of sin
> (O sorrow and shame should this be true!)
> Such giddiness of heart and brain
> Comes seldom save from rage and pain,
> So talks as it's most used to do.
>
> [ll. 673–77]

In a world without imagination, or without dreams, a father's bitterness may come from excess of love, but when dreams intrude, bitterness comes from rage and pain.

Chapter VII

Dejection

"DEJECTION: AN ODE" has the tone of a last poetic utterance. Coleridge is alone speaking of himself, analyzing his own mind, and measuring the distance between his own stifled despair and the joy he hopes is Asra's. There is no other mind whose more joyful experience he can make his own, yet there is no shock or troubled awe at a sudden awareness of his loss. He speaks, in the beginning of the poem, with the settled calm of someone who has long been accustomed to silence and inactivity. And he is roused only by pain. The harp symbol, which he had tried to use as an image of joy in earlier poems, becomes an apt vehicle to express the awakening emotion that moves over him. If he had been able, earlier, to achieve a vicarious joy by overcoming an initial imprisonment, now he begins with the knowledge that he cannot escape; all his effort is concentrated in trying to understand his surroundings.

"Dejection" was first published in the *Morning Post* on October 4, 1802, which was, ironically enough, Wordsworth's wedding day and the seventh anniversary of Coleridge's own marriage. The poem originated, however, in a verse Letter, almost three times as long as the published version, that Coleridge sent to Asra on April 4, 1802.[1] Wordsworth, who had decided to wed Mary Hutchinson and was corresponding with Annette Vallon, the mother of his illegitimate daughter, arrived at Keswick to visit Coleridge on March 28, the day after he had completed the first four stanzas of the "Immortality Ode." Coleridge himself had recently returned to Keswick after an absence of several months. On his way home from London, he visited Asra, a visit which occasioned some unhappiness that is reflected in the Letter.[2]

The Letter itself is almost exclusively concerned with the pain Coleridge believed he caused Asra and with his own domestic unhappiness. He believes that her physical and mental ills were the

[1] The longer April text, which I will refer to as the Letter, was first published by Ernest de Selincourt, "Coleridge's 'Dejection: An Ode,'" *E&S,* 32 (1937), 7–25. It is also available in *CL,* II, 790–98, from which I quote.

[2] An account of these days in March 1802 is contained in *Asra Poems,* p. 42. Coleridge's reaction to the events of the visit is found in *NB,* I, 1150, 1151.

result of "that complaining Scroll / Which even to bodily Sickness bruis'd thy Soul" (Letter, ll. 115–16). Similarly, he attributes the loss of his "shaping Spirit of Imagination" to the receipt of "Ill Tidings" which "bow me down to earth" (Letter, l. 238). The "dark distressful Dream," which in the final version becomes "Reality's dark dream," is not his own agonized self-analysis, but his thoughts about Asra's pain. He wishes for her tranquillity and confesses that he is excluded from peace and joy because of his unhappy marriage with a wife frigidly unsympathetic with his erratic ways. He sees his children as hindrances to his happiness and comes to the terrifying conclusion that at moments he "half-wish'd, they had never been born" (Letter, l. 282).

All references to the "habitual ills" of his relationships with his wife and to the agony of his love for Asra were deleted from the published version. Geoffrey Yarlott believes that the Letter gives a more accurate picture of Coleridge's feelings of guilt than the final "Dejection" and that the Letter points to "the real (rather than the ostensible) cause of Coleridge's breakdown as a poet. For this purpose the autobiographical verse-letter is all-important, since in the Ode the original self-revelation has been camouflaged."[3] There is unquestionably a deep sense of guilt revealed in the Letter, but it is an error to attribute Coleridge's breakdown as a poet to the incidents described in it alone. At most, the trouble with Asra is only symptomatic of a guilt that Coleridge feared was his from his earliest poems. To overlook the evidence of it expressed in "The Ancient Mariner" and "Christabel" and to take as the root cause something that is only one indication of his habitual impulse to distress those whom he loved is to diminish the significance of his insights into the nature of evil and his fears of it. Were it only that he could not, for whatever reason, find for himself the degree of tranquillity he thought he required, then the terror he felt before the evil within him would be reduced to the personal discomfort of an ill and demanding man who can find no sympathy. Furthermore, to place the origin of his feelings of guilt in his relationship with Asra, which began in 1799, is to disregard his earlier anxiety.

While the Letter is primarily concerned with the pain he has caused Asra, "Dejection" is a quite different poem and is concerned almost exclusively with the themes of imagination and loss. The revisions were not just those made to disguise his affair with Asra; he changed the contexts of important passages to emphasize the theme of the loss of imagination. Originally stanzas four and five stood at

[3] Yarlott, p. 248.

the end of the Letter and applied to the blessings he hopes will come to Asra, but in "Dejection" they are transferred to Coleridge's own self-analysis. In the final version they form a part of his introspection and establish the criteria by which he will judge himself, so that when he says "we receive but what we give" (l. 47), the line applies immediately to himself and only indirectly to Asra. The storm, in the Letter, takes his mind off his own inability to respond to nature and makes him think of Asra. Earlier in the Letter, thoughts of her arouse recollections of past joy and bring him some relief:

> I feel my spirit moved—
> And wheresoe'er thou be,
> O Sister! O Beloved!
> Those dear mild Eyes, that see
> Even now the Heaven, *I see*—
> There is a Prayer in them! It is for *me*—
> And I, dear Sara—*I* am blessing *thee*!
>
> [Letter, ll. 92–98]

The Letter is nearer the spirit of the earlier Conversation Poems in that there is an imagined exchange of sympathy, but in "Dejection," he faces a far more fundamental problem. If he himself has lost joy, and if he is the victim of strong feelings, then his blessing could well turn into a curse upon himself and Asra.

The first two stanzas of "Dejection" reflect Coleridge's mood while he gazes at the evening sky, the crescent moon, and the stars: "I see them all so excellently fair, / I see, not feel, how beautiful they are!" (ll. 37–38). He is as removed from their beauty as was the mariner, becalmed on the motionless sea, who "in his loneliness and fixedness ... yearneth towards the journeying Moon." But just as there are other emotions tormenting the mariner, there are other emotions troubling Coleridge. He wrote in a notebook in 1801 that he felt "shipwrecked by storms of doubt, now mastless, rudderless, shattered,—pulling in the dead swell of a dark & windless Sea" (*NB,* I, 932). He thinks in the nautical metaphors of "The Ancient Mariner" and uses the word *rudderless,* one he often used to describe his inability to control the emotion that flowed through him. This entry also anticipates the motto condensed from two stanzas of "The Ballad of Sir Patrick Spence":

> Late, late yestreen I saw the new Moon,
> With the old Moon in her arms;
> And I fear, I fear, My Master dear!
> We shall have a deadly storm.

The conjunction of the new moon with the old reveals the ambiguity of his plight. The new moon promises a new birth and life, but the waning moon was for him a symbol for the curse of death.

The symbol of the moon indicates that Coleridge is isolated from the beauty of the universe, but also that he is not totally devoid of feeling and imagination. The repetition of "I fear, I fear" in the motto characterizes his mood at the beginning of the poem. The moon is an omen that the storm will arrive and bring with it a further awakening of his feelings and imagination, an awakening that by now he sees as a curse. The omen of disaster presented by the moon at first appears to be a relic of superstition, which, in a tone of realistic skepticism, Coleridge regards with detachment. But the presence of the phrase "phantom light" (the phrase is repeated twice), which later becomes a symbol for the radiance of the imagination, suggests that the portent of disaster is to be taken seriously as a prediction of the fate of his imagination. And far from being the curious relic of an ancient superstition, the symbol of the moon predicts that Coleridge's still active imagination may project an image of its own destruction.

Likewise, the symbol of the wind harp indicates that his imagination is not totally unresponsive. Even the tranquil breezes that precede the storm produce a response from the harp, although it is a painful one. Perhaps for him a state of utter insensitivity is better than the slow agony he suffers, but he also knows that he cannot resist the storm's arrival:

> And oh! that even now the gust were swelling,
> And the slant night-shower driving loud and fast!
> Those sounds which oft have raised me, whilst they awed,
> And sent my soul abroad,
> Might now perhaps their wonted impulse give,
> Might startle this dull pain, and make it move and live!
>
> [ll. 15–20]

He has already been forced into a crucial and honest recognition. He knows before the storm comes that it will not elevate his soul and that he will not be able to turn his consciousness outward from the confinements of the self to nature's beauty. It would be safer to be insensitive, but total insensitivity is a death, and he needs the pain to prove that he is alive at all. Both the harp and the moon forecast the perverse freedom of the imagination that brings pain and is inimical to the development of the self. The imprisonment, he feels, is inescapable. The achieved transcendence of his immediate limitations in "This Lime-Tree Bower" and the compensatory hope for Hartley in "Frost at Midnight" are far behind him, and he now can hope only for pain.

Coleridge complains, at the beginning of the second stanza, of a "grief without a pang, void, dark, and drear, / A stifled, drowsy, unimpassioned grief" from which he cannot escape. Before and after his self-analysis, he looks at the storm and finds it merely a mirror of his own mood. Focusing upon that mirror gives him a clearer insight into himself but, ironically, obscures everything outside himself. Thus any outward movement, either to nature or to other minds, is blocked:

> O Lady! in this wan and heartless mood,
> To other thoughts by yonder throstle woo'd,
> All this long eve, so balmy and serene,
> Have I been gazing on the western sky,
> And its peculiar tint of yellow green:
> And still I gaze—and with how blank an eye!
>
> [ll. 25–30]

The lady to whom he confesses is, at this point, an indefinite abstraction, devoid of experience and humanized neither by the necessity of receiving the "wings of healing" that he wishes for her in the last stanza nor by the capability of granting him sympathy, which would encourage him to send his soul to her. Reverting to an earlier form of Conversation Poem, Coleridge places the other mind after the significant experience of the poem, and if there is any shared experience between them, it is that of grief, for which the lady needs the "wings of healing."

Wordsworth observed that Coleridge "had so much acquired the habit of analysing his feelings, and making them matter for a theory or argument, that he had rather dimmed his delight in the beauties of nature."[4] Nature, too, blocks Coleridge's joy because it is not merely nature. The turbulent yellow-green spring storm clouds are both natural phenomena and imaginative constructions. Coleridge insists that whatever we see in nature is a reflection of our own soul, that all of nature's melodies are an echo of our music, and that all of nature's colors are reflections of the self. When he printed lines from "Dejection" in "On the Principles of Genial Criticism," he slightly altered their ordering so as to make a specific identification between the radiant light of joy and the image of the yellow-green clouds:

> Our inmost selves rejoice:
> And thence flows all that glads or ear or sight,
> All melodies the echoes of that voice,

[4] Grosart, III, 427.

All colors a suffusion from that light,
And its celestial tint of yellow-green:
And still I gaze—and with how blank an eye!

[*BL*, II, 240]

The identification of the yellow-green light with the celestial light of joy indicates that to Coleridge the "peculiar tint of yellow green," the moon, and the harp all present the same forecast: all three portend disaster to the imagination, which can respond to pain, but not to beauty, which is merely seen and not felt. Immediately following his use of lines from the "Ode" in "On the Principles of Genial Criticism" he says that "when we declare an object beautiful, the contemplation or intuition of its beauty precedes the *feeling* of complacency, in order of nature at least: nay, in great depression of spirits may even exist without sensibly producing it" (*BL*, II, 241).

Some of the examples Coleridge offers as characteristic of his loss of joy occur earlier, in "Lines Written in the Album at Elbingerode" (1799), composed immediately after a descent of the Brocken.[5] It is organized as a counterstatement to the Conversation Poems and begins with Coleridge's observations from the top of the mountain:

I stood on Brocken's sovran height & saw
Woods crowding upon woods, hills over hills,
A *surging* Scene and only limited
By the blue Distance.

[ll. 1–4]

But the view does not move him and does not become an example of divine creation:

Wearily my way
Downward I dragg'd thro' Fir-groves evermore,
Where bright-green Moss heav'd in sepulchral forms,
Speckled with sunshine; and, but seldom heard,
The sweet Bird's Song became an hollow Sound;
And the Gale murmuring indivisibly
Preserv'd it's solemn murmur most distinct
From many a Note of many a Waterbreak,
And the Brook's *Chatter;* on whose islet stones
The dingy Kidling with it's tinkling Bell
Leapt frolicsome, or old romantic Goat
Sat, his white Beard slow-waving! I mov'd on
With low & languid thought; for I had found
That grandest Scenes have but imperfect Charms,
Where the sight vainly wanders nor beholds

[5] The original version of this poem, which I quote, was sent in a letter to Sara Coleridge (*CL*, I, 504–5).

> One spot, with which the Heart associates
> Holy Remembrances of Child or Friend. . . .
>
> [ll. 4–20]

Separated from the familiar locations and family, he is indifferent to the Brocken's vastness and beauty. He sees the landscape, not as a unity, but as a collection of separate things. The breeze's murmur remains distinct from the notes of the waterfall; even the bird's song is a "hollow Sound." The mood of 1799 is altered in *Sibylline Leaves* (1817) to conform more closely to that of "Dejection." Then he said that "outward forms, the loftiest, still receive / Their finer influence from the Life within" (ll. 17–18).

When he left the mountain, the vision of the Brocken faded "like a departing Dream, / Feeble and dim." But fearing that his mood would appear to be a recantation of his former sublime rhapsodies in other poems, he added, almost parenthetically:

> Stranger! these Impulses
> Blame thou not lightly; nor will *I* profane
> With hasty Judgment or injurious Doubt
> That man's sublimer Spirit, who can feel
> That God is every where!
>
> [ll. 32–36]

In "The Eolian Harp," for instance, he had offered a speculation on God's presence and then rejected it, but on the Brocken he is unmoved by nature and then admits that some persons may be able to see divinity in nature. His intuition of his own difficulty in responding to nature and of his separation from sympathetic friends led him to the conclusion that he was estranged from an active universe.

In the spring of 1802, having found nature only a mirror of his mind, in writing the Letter he was thrust back into himself and into self-analysis to account for his inability to feel nature's beauty:

> My genial spirits fail;
> And what can these avail
> To lift the smothering weight from off my breast?
> It were a vain endeavour,
> Though I should gaze for ever
> On that green light that lingers in the west:
> I may not hope from outward forms to win
> The passion and the life, whose fountains are within.
>
> [ll. 39–46]

The "smothering weight" that oppresses him is the physical sensation of the nightmare. In the last two lines of stanza three and all of stanza four, Coleridge offers the unequivocal generalization that the source of joy is within and only within. And in so asserting he establishes the criteria by which he will judge his incapacity and guilt. He abstracts from his own case, presented by the singular "I" in the third stanza, to all persons. We project a meaning upon nature, and whatever we receive from nature is only a reflection of our minds. Nature's life comes not from an omnipresent spirit but from the soul itself. There is no assertion of the One Life, as Coleridge had previously used the phrase, but he does not reject it for an exclusively projectionist aesthetic.

The lady to whom the poem is addressed, Asra in the Letter, becomes finally the symbol of the proper participation in the active life of the universe. In the closing lines Coleridge prays for her health:

> May all the stars hang bright above her dwelling,
> Silent as though they watched the sleeping Earth!
> With light heart may she rise,
> Gay fancy, cheerful eyes,
> Joy lift her spirit, joy attune her voice;
> To her may all things live, from pole to pole,
> Their life the eddying of her living soul!
>
> [ll. 130–36]

Hers, Coleridge hopes, will be that "shaping spirit of Imagination" which had been his at birth. Yet she will not be the mere passive instrument of an impersonal nature; she will be its spirit, and its life will be the "eddying of her living soul." The standard by which Coleridge judges himself is that of the deified poet, the active soul. The symbols of the mind in stanza four, the light, the glory, and the luminous mist that envelops the earth, all are symbols of the sanctification of the poet. The joy that will be the Lady's and the picture of the deified poet are the most explicit statements of the matured and clarified goal of Coleridge's poetic quest for a substantial self, one in which he is not formed from without but, rather, makes the world in which he lives in the image of his own joy. If the poetic soul can sustain himself and the world around him in this joy, he participates in divinity by acting it. The symbols of deification are neither a palinode nor an announcement of a new projectionist aesthetic. Coleridge never denied belief in a divine reality beyond himself; imagination, genius, and joy were always a means to participate in a common spirit and to approach divine consciousness. Nothing terrified him more than the thought that what he conceived in his mind might not have any corresponding reality. There is no inconsistency in his belief that others could participate in joy and that he could not.

The power possessed by the deified soul is joy. Coleridge associated joy with every aspiration that he had for the development of his self. He informed Sir George Beaumont that the phrase "the joy within me" was "my own Life and my very Self" (*CL*, II, 1053). Joy was not a precondition merely for poetry; it was also the precondition of a harmonious life. The "beautiful and beauty-making power," "Life, and Life's effluence," and "cloud at once and shower"—all refer to a state of being and a process, an action that must be continuously sustained and continually renewed to affirm a harmonious existence. E. H. Coleridge reported that joy for Coleridge was "not mirth or high spirits, or even happiness, but a consciousness of entire and therefore well being, when the emotional and intellectual faculties are in equipoise."[6]

Coleridge judges and finds himself more distant from his goal than ever before. For him the accurate symbol is the harp divested of all the desirable connotations it had possessed for him. What remains is the instrument uttering sounds of pain. The wind, in the opening stanza, "moans and rakes / Upon the strings of this Aeolian lute, / Which better far were mute," and in the seventh stanza the lute sends forth a "scream / Of agony." As he uses it, the harp is an appropriate symbol only for a man incapable of joy, but still capable of partially articulating his grief by thoughts that bring no relief from it. He had been granted joy, but now it is lost, and he is isolated from his former self. Almost paraphrasing the poem in a letter to Beaumont, Coleridge says that joy "was creating me anew to the first purpose of Nature, when other & deeper Distress supervened" (*CL*, II, 1053). The theme of the continuity of the self is an old one for him, and nowhere is there a more painful awareness that the continuous development of the self has been diverted from its original high purpose. "There was a time," he says, when the joy within him "dallied with distress."

Coleridge ascribes his loss of joy to the onset of ill-defined afflictions, which may refer to many particular instances of his domestic unhappiness or to other less definite intimations of the loss of control over himself. The afflictions are "visitations," things that happened to him, emotions, memories, and associations disconnected from an organizing self. They are strong waves of feeling for which abstruse study is an inadequate refuge. Since they come from an unconscious source, he disclaims personal responsibility for them. His self-deception begins when he starts to contradict his earlier assertions that the earth's every hue is a reflection of his own light. It is a

[6] E. H. Coleridge, "The Lake Poets in Somersetshire," *Transactions of the Royal Society of Literature of the United Kingdom*, 2nd ser., 20 (1899), 120.

futile attempt to escape from the "dark dream" of the reality he knows, and it is a measure of the sharp division among his faculties:

> For not to think of what I needs must feel,
>   But to be still and patient, all I can;
> And haply by abstruse research to steal
>   From my own nature all the natural man—
>   This was my sole resource, my only plan:
> Till that which suits a part infects the whole,
> And now is almost grown the habit of my soul.
>
> [ll. 87–93]

In a letter to Southey written in July 1802, Coleridge glossed these lines by saying that "I so attentively watch my own Nature, that my worst Self-delusion is, a compleat Self-knowlege, so mixed with intellectual complacency, that my quickness to see & readiness to acknowlege my faults is too often frustrated by the small pain, which the sight of them gives me, & the consequent slowness to amend them" (*CL,* II, 832).

His loss, as he understands it, is not the result of maturation, as Wordsworth wants to understand his own loss. Wordsworth's aspiration toward a mature tranquillity is based on the remembrances of youthful experiences; Coleridge's "sole resource," an effort to deny his emotions the power to destroy him, is only the substitution of one kind of suicide for another. He tries to quell his natural emotions, not by controlling them and integrating them into his conscious self, but by renouncing them altogether. To deny all emotion, however, is to destroy the natural man. He draws artificial limitations to his self and willfully divides his personality. "Dejection" is a renunciation of his quest.

At the beginning of the poem he had hoped for the arrival of the violent storm, so that he would be awakened into pain. Revivification, he realized, required the torment of his tyrannical passion. But when he considers his particular afflictions, he shifts his expectations, because he has discovered that he needs an opiate to dull his strong feelings. His "sole resource," the "abstruse research" that would prohibit his mind from dwelling upon his emotional instability, he hopes will protect him. The lines explaining his attempts to guard himself from the stormy passions brought him more pain than any others in the poem. Lines eighty-seven to ninety-three were left out of the first printed version in the *Morning Post,* and in the Coleorton manuscript, originally a letter of August 1803 to Sir George Beaumont, the text ends at line eighty-six with the comment "I am so weary of this doleful Poem that I must leave off" (*CL,* II, 973).

While one is usually led to look upon Coleridge's metaphysical studies as his true vocation and avocation, he himself was aware of diverse motives for embarking upon such studies. He knew that his course toward philosophical truth might also be the road to self-forgetfulness. He glossed the phrase "sole resource" in a letter to his brother as "that proud & stoical Apathy, into which I had fallen—it was Resignation indeed, for I was not an Atheist; but it was Resignation—without religion because it was without struggle, without difficulty—because it originated in the Understanding & a stealing Spirit of Contempt, not in the affections" (*CL,* II, 1008). In moments of depression and severe self-criticism, he thought of his metaphysical studies as an irreligious expedient, a non-Christian resignation, that destroyed any possibility of constructing for himself the soul that his metaphysical studies presented as the highest ideal of a purified soul. Coleridge's agony must then have been intensified, for every time he tried to escape his feelings by diverting his attention to philosophy, philosophy and religion presented him with the image of the harmonious soul that he knew he could never realize within himself.

At this painful moment, when he begins to ascribe his loss of joy to causes over which he has no control, he tries to escape the "viper thoughts" of his "dark dream" of self-analysis to something beyond himself. But when he tries to exercise his "sole resource," his attempts bring him face to face with the reality from which he tries to escape. The storm has descended from the mountains and is upon him. He wants to regard it as another of his afflictions. Yet he describes both the torment of self-analysis and the onset of the storm in images he had previously used for the imagination. Both the snake and the harp are images of the imagination that is not a product of joy. They are images of abortive creation, and the imagination here is, as Geoffrey Yarlott has called it, distempered.[7] It is active. The snake has become the viper that strangles him, and the wind is transformed into a "Mad Lutanist" and a "mighty Poet, e'en to frenzy bold," which invades the vernal garden with a wintry blast, destroying life and hope. Coleridge tries to maintain a precarious balance between the knowledge that the storm is a product of his own imagination and the hope that somehow it is an affliction for which he is not responsible. The "fair luminous mist" and the "phantom light" of the new moon have turned into the chaotic storm that terrifies him because although he wants to remain aloof from it, he recognizes it as a mirror of his own soul.

[7] Yarlott, p. 261.

Besides the figure of the wind as the "mighty Poet," there is other evidence that Coleridge recognized that the storm was his own imaginative projection:

> Bare crag, or mountain-tairn, or blasted tree,
> Or pine-grove whither woodman never clomb,
> Or lonely house, long held the witches' home,
> Methinks were fitter instruments for thee. . . .
>
> [ll. 100–103]

Some of the details recall specifically the Brocken, which Coleridge climbed twice during his stay in Germany. Legend has it that, on the evening before May 1 each year, a witches' celebration was held on the summit of the Brocken near what Coleridge described in a letter to his wife as "a sort of Bowling Green inclosed by huge Stones, something like those at Stonehenge; & this is the Witches' Ballroom" (*CL,* I, 504). In the same letter he includes the lines that he had written in the album at Elbingerode, in which he expresses his disappointment and dejection at finding that the "grandest Scenes have but imperfect Charms."

Clement Carlyon reports that both ascents were undertaken, in part at least, to view the specter of the Brocken, an optical phenomenon that had aroused much interest in German scientific journals of the day.[8] At evening or early in the morning when the sun was at the horizon, a shadow from any human form was projected upon the clouds, forming one huge shadow of the perceiver's figure. What may have happened, then, when Coleridge wrote the poem was that he remembered his earlier dejection on the Brocken when the landscape could not elevate his mind to the sublime, a depression similar to that in "Dejection." Then, thinking further of the Brocken, he remembered both the witches' home and the popular lore about the specter of the Brocken and described what he had hoped was the proper home of the storm on the mountain. Since he was fully aware that both the landscape and the specter were projections of his own imagination, he could well have thought of the storm in stanza seven as also the projection of his imagination.

The storm, which he first describes as having all the trappings of popular superstition, the "blasted tree," the "mountain-tairn," the lonely abode of the witches, is not a creation of the mere fancy. It enters the garden and becomes a deadly reality, because its source is not in popular superstition and the idle fancy, but in the uncon-

[8] Clement Carlyon, *Early Years and Late Reflections* (London: Whittaker, 1856), I, 42–50, 170–74. Coleridge copied several of the accounts in his notebooks—see *NB,* I, 430, 431.

trolled fears and the unbridled imagination. From the prediction of the coming storm in the opening stanzas and the consequent self-analysis, the poem returns to the storm. The circle is completed in stanza seven, a circle that excludes other minds and circumscribes Coleridge's own life-in-death.

In the final stanza Coleridge hopes that the storm is "but a mountain-birth," a line that has attracted much attention and many interpretations. House believed that it alluded to Horace's *Ars Poetica:* "Parturient montes, nascetur ridiculus mus" and interpreted it to mean that "what seems to be terrible and destructive may turn out after all to be a mere nothing, or a trifle that cannot disturb" Asra's peace.[9] Schulz argues that House assumes that the poem's subject is the same as that of the Letter: Coleridge's concern with Asra's unhappiness. He contends, on the other hand, that the poem is primarily about the imagination and that almost all the references to the theme of domestic unhappiness have been deleted. In his view, the line is a flaw because he cannot understand how the line applies to Asra as well as to Coleridge himself. There is no evidence in "Dejection" that Asra herself needs the "wings of healing."[10]

If the line is read in reference, not only to Asra, but to Coleridge himself, however, it does make sense. He wishes that the storm's origins are of a "mountain-birth," a source beyond himself. It is an ironically hopeless wish that what appears to be an attribute of the external and natural world is actually such, and not simply the disturbed workings of an imagination that has broken free of conscious control. His fondest wish is that the storm he sees in nature, and half recognizes as his own, will not affect Asra. But he more than suspects that the storm has already invaded her peace as well as his own, so that he prays that sleep will visit her with "wings of healing." In "The Visionary Hope" he strives in vain to be able to receive "some sweet breath of healing" (l. 3). Coleridge and Asra are one mind only in distress.

The prayer for someone else's happiness and the bleak thought that his own is gone are predictable developments of Coleridge's use of the conversational mode in "Dejection." "Frost at Midnight" was revised to approximate the phraseology from "Dejection," as the "Lines Written in the Album at Elbingerode" was revised to approximate its thought. He was able neither to fortify himself against the attacks of strong feelings nor to make them into joyous hopes as he did in his youth. With the possible exception of "To William Words-

[9] House, pp. 165–66.
[10] Schulz, pp. 204–6.

worth," Coleridge was never again to express his most deeply felt thoughts in poetry, for as he said to William Collins in 1818, "Poetry is out of the question. The attempt would only hurry me into that sphere of acute feelings, from which abstruse research, the mother of self-oblivion, presents an asylum" (*CL,* IV, 893). Both asylum and instrument of a willful self-destruction, the "sole resource" represents a dilemma Coleridge met wherever he turned.

Coleridge's ambivalent attitudes toward the feelings are contrasted in two statements made a little more than a year apart, the second after the Letter was written in April 1802. The first is the often-quoted gloss upon "Tintern Abbey," written in February 1801:

—and the deep power of Joy
We see into the *Life* of Things—

i.e.—By deep feeling we make our *Ideas dim*—& this is what we mean by our Life—ourselves. I think of the Wall—it is before me, a distinct Image—here. I necessarily think of the *Idea* & the Thinking I as two distinct & opposite Things. Now let me think of *myself*—of the thinking Being—the Idea becomes dim whatever it be—so dim that I know not what it is—but the Feeling is deep & steady—and this I call *I*—identifying the Percipient & the Perceived—.[11]

But in a letter to William Sotheby written in July 1802, in which Coleridge includes large sections from the April Letter, he proposes the generalization that conceptions colored by strong feelings "as they *recede* from distinctness of *Idea, approximate* to the nature of *Feeling,* & gain thereby a closer & more immediate affinity with the appetites" and that "Suppression & obscurity arrays the simple Truth in a veil of something like Guilt" (*CL,* II, 814). Even though this is a conclusion to a discussion of the propriety of the expression of sexual themes in Theocritus and Salomon Gessner and has little explicit connection with his own condition, it is presented in terms typically Coleridgean. Vivid images rendered dim by strong feelings were for him, but perhaps not for Wordsworth, associated with guilt.

For several occasions when Coleridge made a public statement about the power of the poet to perceive shadows of reality in the particular forms of life, there is a private counterstatement that denies what the more public declaration asserts. In "Apologia Pro Vita Sua" (1800) he portrayed himself as the poet who could envision eternal ideals:

[11] *NB,* I, 921. G. H. G. Orsini believes that the example of the wall may come from Fichte (*Coleridge and German Idealism: A Study in the History of Philosophy* [Carbondale: Southern Illinois Univ. Press, 1969], pp. 178–93).

The poet in his lone yet genial hour
Gives to his eyes a magnifying power:
Or rather he emancipates his eyes
From the black shapeless accidents of size—
In unctuous cones of kindling coal,
Or smoke upwreathing from the pipe's trim bole,
    His gifted ken can see
    Phantoms of sublimity.

This is certainly not Coleridge's best poetry; he is merely playing with the phrase "phantoms of sublimity" and is curious what kind of context he can give it. In an 1805 note he discusses the process by which he imagines that clouds are solid realities, an example of the symbolic process of creating realities from the airy nothings of his mind, and he dismisses these creations as "'*phantoms* of Sublimity' which I continue to know to be *phantoms*" (*NB,* II, 2402). In "Phantom" (1805) he imagines an "abstract Self" which is a "Universal personified":

All look and likeness caught from earth,
All accident of kin and birth,
Had pass'd away. There was no trace
Of aught on that illumined face,
Uprais'd beneath the rifted stone
But of one spirit all her own;—
She, she herself, and only she,
Shone through her body visibly.

Yet in the Malta notebook in which this is glossed as the "*universal-in-particularness* of Form," he laments the "seldomness of the Feeling" (*NB,* II, 2441).

These are only a few of the instances when he admitted that he had failed to create a unified self. The man of genius, the man who can allow his unconscious to contribute to his knowledge, he wrote in "On Poesy or Art," must "eloign himself from nature in order to return to her with full effect" and must "out of his own mind create forms according to the severe laws of the intellect." The poet's creations, his "living and life-producing ideas," share a common substantiality with nature; his ideas are "essentially one with the germinal causes in nature—his consciousness being the focus and mirror of both." The movement of consciousness is similar to that which Coleridge attempted in "This Lime-Tree Bower" and "Frost at Midnight," but in those poems he began in an involuntary exile from nature, to which he attempts to return. He insists that this movement from the life within to the life without is the only acceptable alternative; the other is the "dreary (and thank heaven! almost impossible) belief that every thing around us is but a phantom" (*BL,* II, 258–59). Doubtless the source of this explanation is as much his own experience as his philosophical studies and his use of Schelling's words.

Early in January 1807 Wordsworth finished reading to Coleridge the completed draft of *The Prelude,* a poem which reminded Coleridge that Wordsworth was the man of genius and that he was not. He had publicly maintained from the moment of their first meeting that Wordsworth was "a *good* and *kind* man, & the only one whom in *all* things I feel my Superior" (*CL,* I, 491). The poem Coleridge wrote in response to the reading, "To William Wordsworth," contains the ideal of the integrated personality as Coleridge conceived of it. Wordsworth was aware, as much as it was possible to be aware, of the continuousness of his identity:

> Of thy own spirit thou hast loved to tell
> What *may* be told, by words revealable;
> With heavenly breathings, like the secret soul
> Of vernal growth, oft quickening in the heart,
> Thoughts that obey no mastery of words,
> Pure self-beholdings!
>
> [*PW,* I, 404; MS. B]

What Wordsworth possessed, and Coleridge did not, was the creative memory and the consciousness that the experiences of childhood could be assimilated into those of the adult. As Hazlitt was to say later in his *Table Talk,* Wordsworth "contemplates a whole-length figure of himself, he looks along the unbroken line of his personal identity."[12]

Coleridge's enumeration of Wordsworth's youthful joys constitutes his own wish that he too had been able to participate in such joys. Similarly, his re-creation of Wordsworth's separation from innocence and his crisis in France is a re-creation of his own crisis:

> France in all her towns lay vibrating
> Like some becalmèd bark beneath the burst
> Of Heaven's immediate thunder, when no cloud
> Is visible, or shadow on the main.
>
> [ll. 29–32]

The picture of Wordsworth becalmed and plagued by thunder from a cloudless sky is also Coleridge's of the mariner in the depths of the nightmare. Coleridge admires Wordsworth, not only because he is the imaginative man, but especially because he can weather the crisis

[12] Hazlitt, VIII, 44.

and return to the "dread watch-tower of man's absolute self" (l. 40) and achieve an enduring permanence:

> Ere yet that last strain dying awed the air,
> With stedfast eye I viewed thee in the choir
> Of ever-enduring men. The truly great
> Have all one age, and from one visible space
> Shed influence! They, both in power and act,
> Are permanent, and Time is not with them,
> Save as it worketh for them, they in it.
>
> [ll. 48–54]

From his own point of view, Coleridge at times saw *The Prelude* as being about the growth of Wordsworth's capability to withdraw into his inner strength and to endure. Wordsworth was for Coleridge a symbol of endurance to whom he turned in his hopes for Asra's peace in the Letter:

> To all things I prefer the Permanent.
> And better seems it for a heart, like mine,
> Always to *know,* than sometimes to behold,
> *Their* Happiness & thine—
> For Change doth trouble me with pangs untold!
> To see thee, hear thee, feel thee—then to part
> Oh!—it weighs down the Heart!
> To *visit* those, I love, as I love thee,
> Mary, & William, & dear Dorothy,
> It is but a temptation to repine—
> The transientness is Poison in the Wine,
> Eats out the pith of Joy, makes all Joy hollow,
> All Pleasure a dim Dream of Pain to follow!
>
> [Letter, ll. 150–62]

It may not have been only Chatterton of whom Wordsworth was thinking when he wrote in "Resolution and Independence," composed a few weeks after Coleridge had written the Letter, "We Poets in our youth begin in gladness; / But thereof come in the end despondency and madness" (ll. 48–49).

As Coleridge listens to the reading of *The Prelude,* pulses of feeling begin to revive in him as though he were a drowned man returning to life. The returning life, however, brings him only a "throng of pains" (l. 64), just as the storm in "Dejection" brings the storm of pain. His youth, manhood, genius, and knowledge were in vain. The foliage which he ascribed in "Dejection" to his youthful hopes are here "but flowers / Strewed on my corse, and born upon my bier" (ll. 73–74). Coleridge may be answering directly Wordsworth's address to him in Book VI of *The Prelude:*

I have thought
Of Thee, thy learning, gorgeous eloquence,
And all the strength and plumage of thy youth,
Thy subtle speculations, toils abstruse
Among the Schoolmen, and platonic forms
Of wild ideal pageantry, shap'd out
From things well-match'd, or ill, and words for things,
The self-created sustenance of a mind
Debarr'd from Nature's living images,
Compell'd to be a life unto itself,
And unrelentingly possess'd by thirst
Of greatness, love, and beauty.

[1805; ll. 305–16]

Coleridge interrupts his self-pitying strain with the phrase "That way no more" (l. 76), as abrupt a change of course as he makes in "Dejection" with the phrase "Hence, viper thoughts." He assures himself that Wordsworth will gain peace: "Amid the howl of more than wintry storms, / The Halcyon hears the voice of vernal hours / Already on the wing" (ll. 89–91). The April storm that descended from the mountain in "Dejection" is a "worse than wintry song." As in "Dejection," where he hopes that Asra will be visited with joy, his only consolation here is in contemplating joys he cannot share.

"To William Wordsworth" is the last of Coleridge's poems called conversational. His later poetry, when it approaches personal themes, as in "The Visionary Hope," is a dialogue of self and hollow echo. There is no place for the vitality of other minds in the self-created limbo where "Time and weary Space / Fettered from flight, with night-mare sense of fleeing, / Strive for their last crepuscular half-being" ("Limbo," ll. 12–14). In a limbo his abode is

Wall'd round, and made a spirit-jail secure,
By the mere horror of blank Naught-at-all,
Whose circumambience both these ghosts enthral.
A lurid thought is growthless, dull Privation,
Yet that is but a Purgatory curse;
Hell knows a fear far worse,
A fear—a future state;—'tis positive Negation!

[ll. 32–38]

The mind-created walls permit no utterance that would bring relief. They exclude the permanence of joy and include the persistent phantom, the self-consciousness which John Stuart Mill called "the daemon of the men of genius of our time."[13]

[13] *On Bentham and Coleridge,* ed. with an Introduction by F. R. Leavis (New York: Harper, 1962), p. 62.

Coleridge's final statement on his quest to know his self may well be the last lines of "Self-Knowledge," written two years before he died:

What is there in thee, Man, that can be known?—
Dark fluxion, all unfixable by thought,
A phantom dim of past and future wrought,
Vain sister of the worm,—life, death, soul, clod—
Ignore thyself, and strive to know thy God!

[ll. 6–10]

Appendix
Index

Appendix

"Effusion XXXV" from *Poems on Various Subjects* (1796)

Effusion XXXV.

COMPOSED
August 20th, 1795,
AT CLEVEDON, SOMERSETSHIRE

My pensive Sara! thy soft cheek reclin'd
Thus on mine arm, most soothing sweet it is
To sit beside our cot, our cot o'er grown
With white-flower'd Jasmin, and the broad-leav'd Myrtle,
(Meet emblems they of Innocence and Love!)
And watch the clouds, that late were rich with light,
Slow sad'ning round, and mark the star of eve
Serenely brilliant (such should Wisdom be)
Shine opposite! How exquisite the scents
Snatch'd from yon bean-field! and the world *so* hush'd!
The stilly murmur of the distant Sea
Tells us of Silence. And that simplest Lute
Plac'd length-ways in the clasping casement, hark!
How by the desultory breeze caress'd,
Like some coy Maid half-yielding to her Lover,
It pours such sweet upbraidings, as must needs
Tempt to repeat the wrong! And now its strings
Boldlier swept, the long sequacious notes
Over delicious surges sink and rise,
Such a soft floating witchery of sound
As twilight Elfins make, when they at eve
Voyage on gentle gales from Faery Land,
Where *Melodies* round honey-dropping flowers
Footless and wild, like birds of Paradise,
Nor pause nor perch, hov'ring on untam'd wing.

And thus, my Love! as on the midway slope
Of yonder hill I stretch my limbs at noon
Whilst thro' my half-clos'd eyelids I behold
The sunbeams dance, like diamonds, on the main,
And tranquil muse upon tranquillity;

Full many a thought uncall'd and undetain'd,
And many idle flitting phantasies,
Traverse my indolent and passive brain
As wild and various, as the random gales
That swell or flutter on this subject Lute!
And what if all of animated nature
Be but organic Harps diversly fram'd,
That tremble into thought, as o'er them sweeps,
Plastic and vast, one intellectual Breeze,
At once the Soul of each, and God of all?
But thy more serious eye a mild reproof
Darts, O beloved Woman! nor such thoughts
Dim and unhallow'd dost thou not reject,
And biddest me walk humbly with my God.

Meek Daughter in the Family of Christ,
Well hast thou said and holily disprais'd
These shapings of the unregenerate mind,
Bubbles that glitter as they rise and break
On vain Philosophy's aye-babbling spring.
For never guiltless may I speak of Him,
Th' INCOMPREHENSIBLE! save when with awe
I praise him, and with Faith that inly* *feels;*
Who with his saving mercies healed me,
A sinful and most miserable man
Wilder'd and dark, and gave me to possess
PEACE, and this COT and THEE, heart-honor'd Maid!

*L'athée n'est point à mes yeux un faux esprit; je puis vivre avec lui aussi bien et mieux qu'avec le dévot, car il raisonne davantage, mais il lui manque un sens, et mon ame ne se fond point entièrement avec la sienne: il est froid au spectacle le plus ravissant, et il cherche un syllogisme lorsque je rends une action de grace.

"Appel a l'impartiale postérité", par la Citoyenne Roland, troisieme partie, p. 67.

Index